THE

CANCELLED

ARGYLL

THE GLENS
OF ARGYLL

A personal survey of the Glens of Argyll

for mountainbikers and walkers

by

Peter D. Koch-Osborne

CICERONE PRESS
MILNTHORPE CUMBRIA

© P. D. Koch-Osborne 1996
ISBN 1 85284 226 1

British Library Cataloguing-in-Publication Data.
A catalogue record of this book is
available from the British Library.

Just as long as there's somewhere
left to walk, to sit, to cycle,
And something left to look at.
                    D. J. Enright
                    (Penguin Dictionary
                        of Quotations)

Cover pictures :- Loch Etive

Index

Introduction

Access to the tracks on the following pages can rarely be regarded as an absolute right by the cyclist or walker. Almost all land is private and it is often only the good nature of the owners that allows us to travel unhindered over his land. In Scottish law the term trespass implies nuisance or damage. In practice sensible conduct removes any possibility of nuisance. Respect the grouse season (12 Aug to 10 Dec) and deer stalking (1 Jul to 20 Oct - stags and 21 Oct to 15 Feb - hinds). Your author has not once met with animosity in meeting 'keepers. Your good conduct will ensure continued access. Cyclists - stay on the trail and slow down!!

Conservation of the wild areas of Scotland is of paramount importance. Much has been written elsewhere but users of this guide must appreciate that the very ground over which you walk or cycle will be damaged if care is not taken. Please don't use a bike on soft peat paths and tread carefully on other than a stony track. Many of the tracks are in themselves an eyesore and any "development" can cause irreparable damage. Make sure, as walkers and cyclists, we encourage the conservation of our wilderness areas without the pressure of our activities causing further damage. In publishing this book a great deal of trust is placed upon you, the reader, to respect the needs of the region. If all you need is exercise - go to a sports centre! but if you appreciate the unique qualities of the wild places they are yours to enjoy..... carefully! Careless conduct not only damages what we seek to enjoy but, equally seriously, gives landowners good reason to restrict access.

The Maps on the following pages give sufficient detail for exploration of the glens but the Ordnance Survey Landranger maps of the region should also be used if the full geographical context of the area is to be fully appreciated. These maps and the knowledge of their proper use are essential if a long tour or cross country route is to be undertaken.

The mountain bike, or ATB - all terrain bike, has in the author's opinion been badly named. It does not belong on the high tops but is ideal in the glens covering at least twice the distance of the average walker, quietly, whilst still allowing a full appreciation of the surroundings and providing further exploration into the wilderness especially on short winter days. The bike must be a well maintained machine complete with a few essential spares as a broken bike miles from anywhere can be serious. Spare gear is best carried in strong panniers on good carriers. Poor quality bikes and accessories simply will not last. Front panniers help distribute weight and prevent "wheelies". Mud-guards are essential. Heavy rucksacks are tiring and put more weight onto one's already battered posterior! The brightly coloured "high profile" image of mountainbiking is unsuited to the remote glens. These wild areas are sacred and need treating as such.

Clothing for the mountainbiker is an important consideration, traditional road cycling gear is un-suitable. High ankle trainers are best for summer, and light weight walking boots for winter cycling. A zipped fleece jacket with waterproof top and overtrousers with spare thin sweatshirts etc should be included for easily adjusting temperature. The wearing of a helmet is a personal choice, it depends how you ride, where you ride and the value you place on your head! In any event a thin balaclava will be required under a helmet in winter or a thick one in place of a helmet. Good waterproof gloves are essential. Fingers and ears get painfully cold on a long descent at -5°C. Protection against exposure should be as for mountain walking. Many of the glens are as high as English hilltops. The road cyclist's shorts or longs will keep legs warm in summer only. In winter walker's breeches and overtrousers are more suitable.

Clothing for the walker has had much written about it elsewhere. Obviously full waterproofs, spare warm clothing, spare food etc. should be included. In winter conditions the longer through routes should never be attempted alone or by the inexperienced.

Mountainbikers and walkers alike should never be without a good map, this book (!), a whistle (and knowledge of its proper use), compass, emergency rations, and in winter a sleeping bag and cooker may be included even if an overnight stop is not planned. Word of your planned route should be left together with your estimated time of arrival. The bothies must be left tidy with firewood for the next visitor. Don't be too proud to remove someone else's litter. Join the Mountain Bothies Association to help support the maintenance of these simple shelters. It should not be necessary to repeat the Country Code and the Mountain Bike Code, the true lover of the wild places needs peace and space - not rules and regulations.

River crossings are a major consideration when planning long or "through" routes virtually anywhere in Scotland. It must be remembered that snowmelt from the high mountains can turn what is a fordable stream in early morning into a raging torrent by mid afternoon. Walkers should hold on to each other, in three's, forming a triangle if possible. Rivers can be easier to cross with a bike, as the bike can be moved, brakes applied, leant on, then the feet can be re-positioned and so on. The procedure is to remove boots and socks, replace boots, make sure you can't drop anything and cross - ouch! Drain boots well, dry your feet and hopefully your still dry socks will help to warm your feet up. Snowmelt is so cold it hurts. Choose a wide shallow point to cross and above all don't take risks.

Ascents on a bike should be tackled steadily in a very low gear and sitting down wherever possible. While front panniers prevent "wheelies" sitting down helps the rear wheel grip. Standing on the pedals causes wheel slip, erosion, and is tiring. Pushing a laden mountainbike is no fun and usually the result of tackling the lower half of a climb standing up, in the wrong gear or too fast.

Descents on a bike can be exhilarating but a fast descent is hard on the bike, the rider, and erodes the track if wheels are locked. It is also ill-mannered towards others who may be just around the next bend.

Last but not least other users of the tracks need treating with respect - it may be the owner! Bad conduct can only lead to restricted access, spoiling it for us all.

The Maps 1

The maps are drawn to depict the most important features to the explorer of the glens. North is always at the top of each map and all maps, apart from the detail sketches, are to the same scale :- 1km or 0.6 miles being shown on each map. An attempt has been made to present the maps in a pictorially interesting way. A brief explanation of the various features is set out below :-

<u>Tracks</u> :- One of the prime objects of this book is to grade the tracks according to "roughness". This information is essential to the mountainbiker and useful to the walker. With due respect to the Ordnance Survey one "other road, drive or track" can take twice as long to cycle along as another yet both may be depicted in the same way. The author's attempt at grading is set out below :-

 metalled road, not too many fortunately, public roads are generally included only to locate the start of a route.

 good track, hardly rutted, nearly as fast as a road to cycle on but can be boring to walk far on. Most are forest tracks.

the usual rutted "Landrover" track, rough but all easily rideable on a mountainbike, not too tedious to walk on.

 rough, very rutted track nearly all rideable, can be very rough even for walking. Either very stony or overgrown or boggy.

walker's path, usually over 50% is rideable and included especially as a part of a through route. Details given on each map.

<u>Relief</u> is depicted in two ways. The heavy black lines are now a commonly used method of depicting main mountain summits, ridges and spurs thus:-

Contour lines are also used, at 50m intervals up to about 600m. This adds "shape" to the glens as mapped and gives the reader an idea of how much climbing is involved. Reference to the gradient profiles at the start of each section compares the various routes:-

500 m   550 m   600 m

<u>Crags</u> in the high mountains are shown thus:-

....with major areas of scree shown dotted

<u>Rivers</u> generally "uncrossable" are shown as two lines whilst streams, generally "crossable" are shown using a single line. Note:- great care is needed crossing even the larger streams. Falling in can cause embarrassment at best, exposure or drowning at worst. Please don't take risks - besides you'd get this book wet !!

loch or lochan

<u>Buildings</u> and significant ruins are shown as a:- ◼

<u>Bridges</u> are rather obviously shown thus:- ⟩⟨ There are so many trees I wish there were an easier way of drawing them -but there isn't! I'm fed up with drawing trees!!

etc etc.....

The Glens of Argyll - North

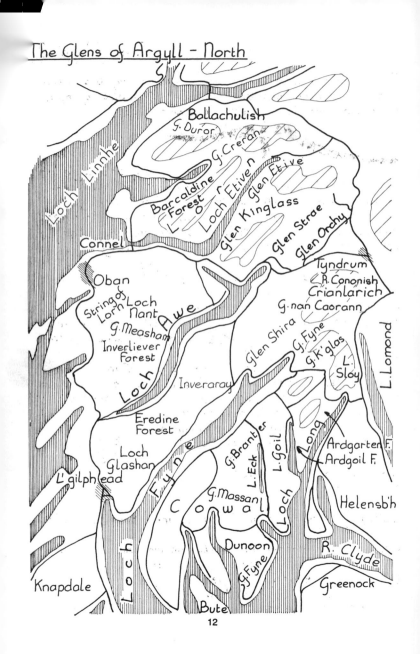

Map of The Glens of Argyll showing land over 600m or 2000ft. A more detailed map of each area precedes each section :- 'Lorn', 'Oban to Inveraray', 'East of Loch Awe and Cowal', and 'Knapdale and Kintyre'. Feasible through or 'link' routes are given in the final section of this book.

Crinan Canal

Lochgilphead

Knapdale F.

Cowal

Knapdale

Loch Garasdale

Gleann Drochaide

Glen Lussa

Campbeltown

Strone Glen

Mull of Kintyre

Lorn

Lorn

Access:- The area covered in this section lies north of the Tyndrum to Oban road and west of the Tyndrum to Ballachulish road. The area is encircled by these, and the less busy coast road, making access to most routes easy by car. Indeed its proximity to major routes and centres of population in Scotland's "Central Belt" make this scenic area deservedly popular, tempered only by rain and midges! The railways from Tyndrum to Oban and to Bridge of Orchy open up through route possibilities putting many of these within weekend distance of Glasgow, even using public transport.

Accommodation:- The perimeter of the area is well served with all types of accommodation, from campsites to hotels. The interior of the region is however almost devoid of anywhere to stay other than to camp "wild". Tourist information centres are located in Oban (open all year) and Tyndrum and Ballachulish (both Apr.-Oct.) There are Youth Hostels at Oban, Glencoe and Crianlarich.

Geographical Features:- An area of high mountains and fjord-like sea lochs yet so accessible! Many of the glens are now carpeted with commercial forest, indeed Glen Orchy seems to be disappearing under a thick blanket of trees. The infamous high rainfall of the region results in many small burns becoming major rivers within 10 miles of their origin, yet the routes given in the following pages avoid major fords as, unlike some areas, the provision of bridges is excellent.

Mountains:- The Glencoe mountains lie across the north of the region; this serious mountain area is for the climber and very experienced hillwalker only. Many walkers have become sad statistics taking to the hills in the vicious weather winter throws against them. The names Bidean, Buachaille Etive Mor and Stob Coire nan Lochan are music to the climber's ears, because of (and not despite) the dangers and challenges they offer. Further south the less well known Ben Starav and the very well known Ben Cruachan are but two among many fine peaks. The pumped storage hydro-electric scheme on Cruachan is now a day trip tourist attraction. Such a dignified mountain surely deserves better than to have coach loads of people gawping at its wounds.

Rivers:- The Coe drains the northern mountains whilst the Orchy and Awe drain the south. The heart of the region is drained by the rivers Duror, Creran, Etive, Kinglass and Strae which follow the glaciated glens of the routes described.

Forests:- There is little of interest besides the vast commercial forests, which do indeed provide some good tracks. However, dense planting to a straight edge puts an element of order and regimentation into the natural scene which never looks right.

Lochs:- Lochs Linnhe, Creran and Etive are all sea lochs. The area touches on the fresh waters of Loch Tulla, which really belongs to Rannoch and onto Loch Awe which resides in the next section of this book. So, apart from L. Dochard in Glen Kinglass and a few puddles there is surprisingly little fresh water in Lorn.

Emergency:- Only the Kinglass watershed can be described as remote from habitation or road. A wary eye on the weather should avoid any trouble in route finding. Otherwise, contact with civilisation is never far away.

Lorn Routes 1

Barcaldine Forest

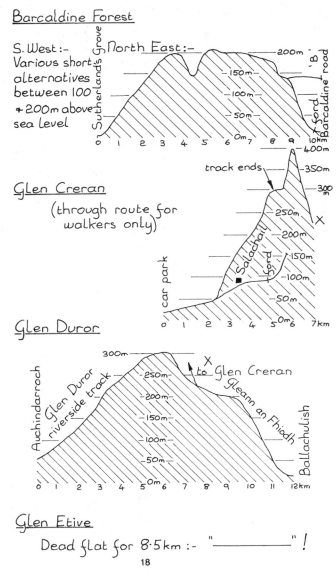

S. West:-
Various short
alternatives
between 100
+ 200m above
sea level

North East:-

Glen Creran

(through route for walkers only)

track ends

Glen Duror

Glen Etive

Dead flat for 8·5km :- "——————" !

18

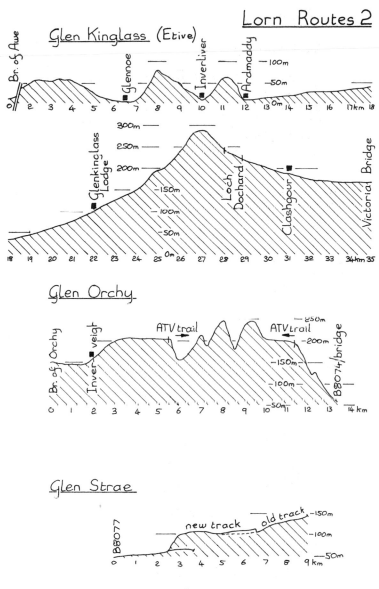

Lorn Routes 2

Glen Kinglass (Etive)

Glen Orchy

Glen Strae

19

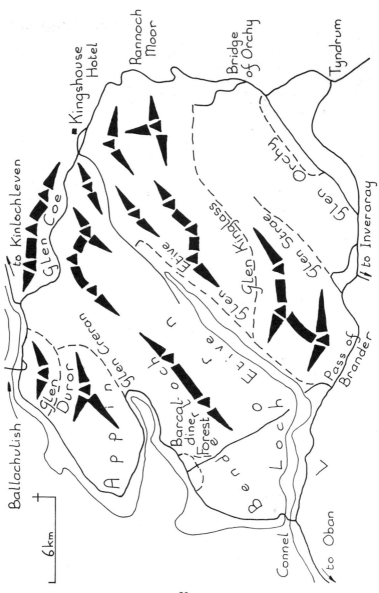

Ballachulish

to Kinlochleven

Glen Coe

Kingshouse Hotel

Rannoch Moor

Bridge of Orchy

Tyndrum

to Inveraray

Glen Orchy

Glen Strae

Glen Kinglass

Glen Etive

Glen Creran

Glen Duror

Appin

Barcaldine Forest

Loch Etive

Pass of Brander

Ben Loch

Connel

to Oban

6 km

20

Barcaldine Forest straddles Gleann Salach up which the 'B' road to Bonawe dissects the forest into two distinct areas. The south west acts as an extension to the north eastern area, which accommodates the car park at Sutherland's Grove and also provides the best tracks - around Gleann Dubh and its reservoir. Forest Enterprise have laid out marked trails for cyclists and shorter paths for walkers but the maps on these two pages allow various self-planned sorties into the forest. The higher tracks boast good views despite the trees. The remainder of the tracks are pleasant, if unremarkable.

old rly.

Sutherland's Grove car park.

Loch Creran

Barcaldine

Continued Barcaldine Forest 2

gate

to Benderloch 4km/2.5m

Achinreir

50 m

150 m

gate

100 m

200 m

224m

Dubh Loch Mor

200

N

1km

250 m

Sgorr a Mham-lic

21

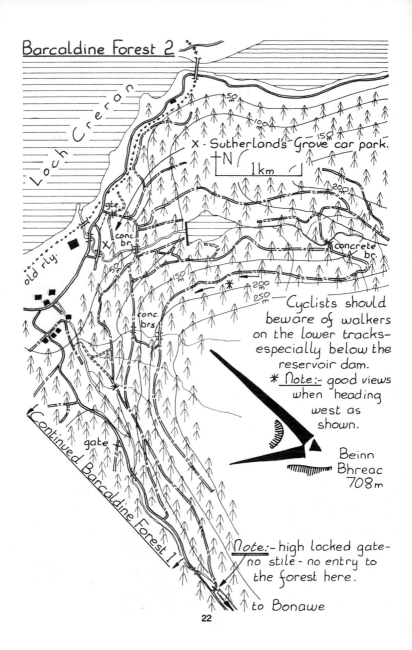

Barcaldine Forest 2

Loch Creran

old rly.

X - Sutherland's Grove car park.

gate

conc. br.

conc. brs.

concrete br.

N 1km

150 m

100 m

150 m

200 m

150 m

200 m
250 m

Cyclists should beware of walkers on the lower tracks- especially below the reservoir dam.
* Note:- good views when heading west as shown.

Beinn Bhreac 708m

gate

Continued Barcaldine Forest 1

Note:- high locked gate- stile - no entry to the forest here.

to Bonawe

22

Glen Creran runs inland from the head of Loch Creran, justifying the tortuous route of the main road around the loch, by giving a reason to halt at its head. The Oban-Ballachulish railway took a short cut over the narrows at <u>Dallachulish</u>. Your author recalls only too well a cycle ride from Loch Lochy to Oban, via Loch Eil, against a strong south-westerly when the Loch Creran diversion seemed grossly unfair! Anyway, we now explore the glen and its pedestrian links to the Glen Duror/Gleann an Fhiodh path which provide through walks to Auchindarroch in the west and Ballachulish in the north. There is no shelter. Distances below in km and (miles).

location map

A glimpse through the trees from the higher section of the link path to Glen Duror.

Glen Creran 2

The route is 'cycleable' to 'X', the start of the Link path, and Y, the ford. There is no point crossing the ford as the short track on the far side is not worth wet feet!

◀Continued Glen Duror 2

▲Continued Glen Duror 3▶

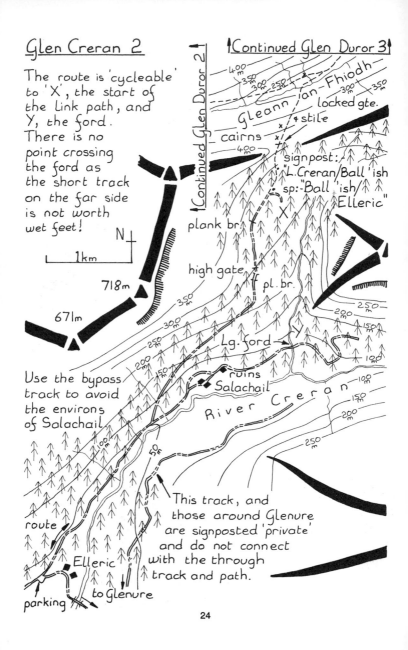

N↑

1km

718m

671m

Gleann an-Fhiodh

locked gte.

stile

cairns

signpost: "L.Creran/Ball 'ish"

sp:-"Ball 'ish/ Elleric"

X

plank br.

high gate

pl. br.

Lg. ford →

ruins Salachail

River Creran

Use the bypass track to avoid the environs of Salachail

route

Elleric

parking

to Glenure

This track, and those around Glenure are signposted 'private' and do not connect with the through track and path.

Glen Duror, together with Gleann an Fhiodh forms an off-road link from Auchindarroch to Ballachulish with a southern link to Glen Creran. Though just passable on a bike the path in Gleann an Fhiodh is best tackled south-west to north-east, ie - downhill. The through route does, however make a fine walk.

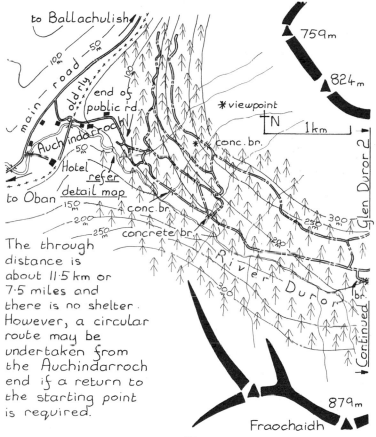

to Ballachulish

100
50

old rly

main road

end of public rd.

Auchindarroch

50

Hotel

refer detail map

to Oban

150 m
200 m
250 m

conc. br.

concrete br.

759 m

824 m

*viewpoint

N   1 km

conc. br.

250 m   300 m

280

River Duror

300

879 m

Fraochaidh

Glen Duror 2

Continued

The through distance is about 11·5 km or 7·5 miles and there is no shelter. However, a circular route may be undertaken from the Auchindarroch end if a return to the starting point is required.

Glen Duror 2

The environs of Auchindarroch

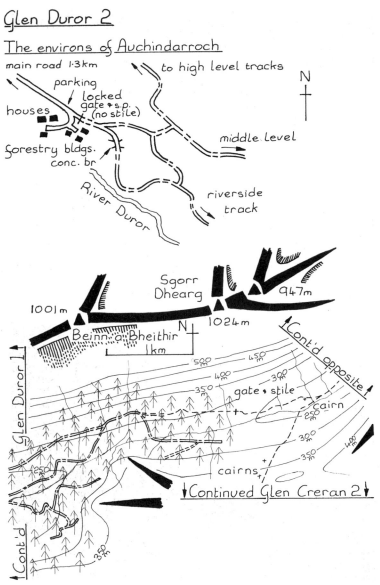

main road 1·3km

to high level tracks

N

parking

locked gate & s.p. (no stile)

houses

Forestry bldgs.
conc. br

middle level

River Duror

riverside track

Sgorr Dhearg

947m

1001m

1024m

Beinn a Bheithir

N

1km

Glen Duror 1

Cont'd opposite

500 450 400 350 300

gate & stile

cairn

250

300

400

350

cairns

Continued Glen Creran 2

250

350

Cont'd

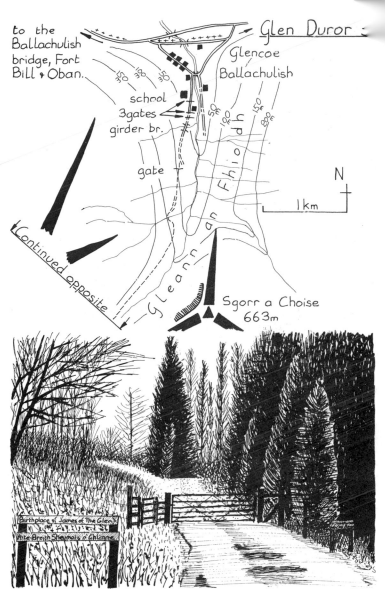

to the Ballachulish bridge, Fort Bill & Oban.

Glen Duror

Glencoe
Ballachulish

150
30
50

school
3 gates
girder br.

gate

50
100
150
200

Gleann an Fhiodh

N

1 km

Continued opposite

Sgorr a Choise
663m

Birthplace o James of The Glen
Aite-Breith Sheumais a' Ghlinne

en Etive 1

This section covers the south east side of the head of Loch Etive, a walk of some 13km (8·5m) each way (to Ardmaddy). This route is supplementary to the Loch Etive (south west) to Glen Kinglass through route. Unlike Glen Kinglass, however, this is not a cycle ride, being too rough and wet. The path, in the shadow of Ben Starav is a fine walk which can be turned into a long trek via either Glen Kinglass or by continuing via Loch Etive to Bridge of Awe. The right-of-way along the north west side of Loch Etive is not included in this book as, unfortunately, the quarry at Bon-awe restricts access. It is also an eyesore. There is limited shelter along the lochside (none when this falls down). Farms at Ardmaddy and south west of same are occupied. Study with care the long distances relating to these routes as set out below - before setting off. For those fit enough the rewards are great.

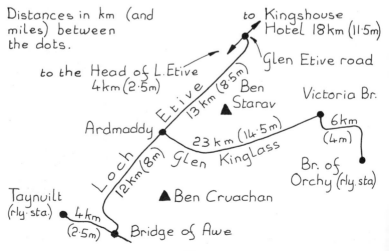

Distances in km (and miles) between the dots.

to Kingshouse Hotel 18km (11·5m)

Glen Etive road

to the Head of L.Etive 4km (2·5m)

13km (8·5m)

Loch Etive

Ben Starav

Victoria Br.

Ardmaddy

23 km (14·5m)

Glen Kinglass

12km (8m)

6km (4m)

Br. of Orchy (rly. sta.)

Ben Cruachan

Taynuilt (rly. sta.)

4km (2·5m)

Bridge of Awe

28

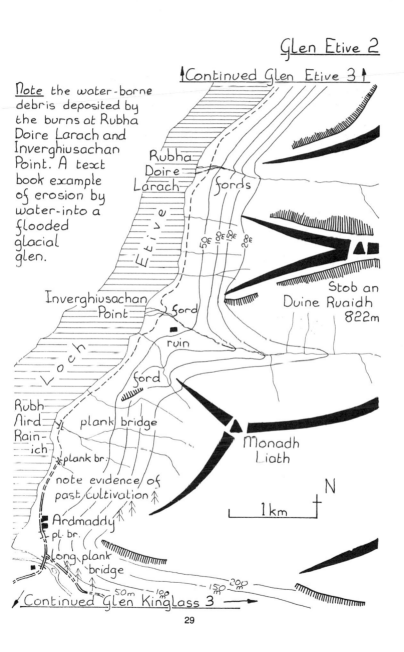

Note the water-borne debris deposited by the burns at Rubha Doire Larach and Inverghiusachan Point. A text book example of erosion by water-into a flooded glacial glen.

Rubha Doire Larach

fords

Etive

50m 100m 150m 200m

Stob an Duine Ruaidh 822m

Inverghiusachan Point

ford

ruin

Loch

ford

Rubh Aird Rainich

plank bridge

Monadh Liath

plank br.

note evidence of past cultivation

N

1 km

Ardmaddy

pl. br.

long plank bridge

50m 100m 150m 200m

← Continued Glen Kinglass 3 →

29

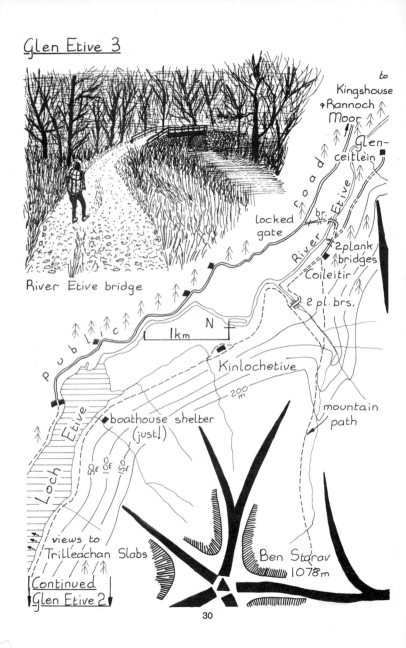

Glen Etive 3

to
Kingshouse
& Rannoch
Moor

Glen-
ceitlein

Road

River Etive

locked
gate

br.

2 plank
bridges

Coileitir

2 pl. brs.

River Etive bridge

N

1km

Kinlochetive

200 m

mountain
path

Public

Loch Etive

boathouse shelter
(just!)

300

views to
Trilleachan Slabs

Continued
Glen Etive 2

Ben Starav
1078m

Glen Kinglass is a classic long through route ideally suited to both the long distance walker and off-road cyclist. The track is never tedious to walk upon, nor is it too rough to negotiate with a bike. New vistas open up at every turn in the trail from sea-loch to a route through the heart of the mountains. If the outdoor man (or woman) cannot enjoy Glen Kinglass it is surely time to pack it in! This is however a long route requiring a good standard of fitness; refer to the distance map on Glen Etive 1 which also reveals the walking (only) option to the public road in Glen Etive. The through route possibilities for the walker are enhanced by the railway stations at Taynuilt and Bridge of Orchy, whilst the cyclist may prefer the long circular ride via Glen Orchy and Loch Awe. This is best done clockwise completing the busy Pass of Brander early in the morning and ending up with either the quiet public road down Glen Orchy or the demanding forest trail — the next route in this guide. This is a round trip of 82 km or about 51 miles (allow 10 hours). Further extended tours are possible as the Glen Kinglass track meets both the West Highland Way and Water of Tulla at Victoria Bridge.* There is emergency shelter at Narrachan, and Glennoe, Inverliver, Ardmaddy, Glenkinglass Lodge and Clashgour are normally all occupied.

*Refer to Book 3 "The Glens of Rannoch".

<u>Note:-</u> Study of older maps reveals that the only vehicular access to Ardmaddy was via Victoria Br. The Br. of Awe track is a later addition. Access to Inverliver and Glennoe was by boat or on foot.

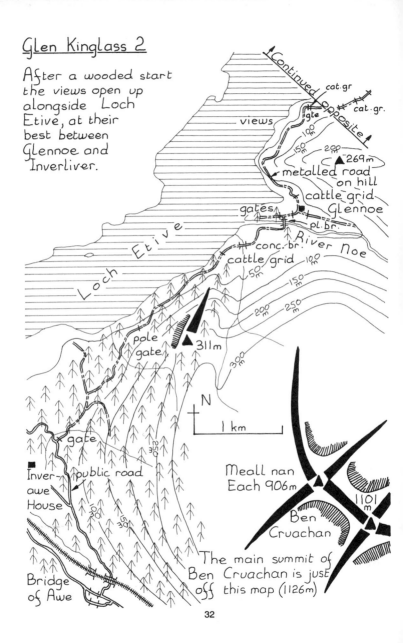

Glen Kinglass 2

After a wooded start
the views open up
alongside Loch
Etive, at their
best between
Glennoe and
Inverliver.

Continued opposite

cat. gr.

cat. gr.

views

gte

100m

150m

200m

▲ 269m

metalled road
on hill

cattle grid

Glennoe

gates

pl. br.

River Noe

conc. br.

cattle grid

50m

100m

150m

200m

250m

300m

pole
gate

▲ 311m

N

1 km

✗ gate

Inver-
awe
House

public road

50m
100m
150m

250m
350m

Meall nan
Each 906m

1101
m

Ben
Cruachan

Bridge
of Awe

The main summit of
Ben Cruachan is just
off this map (1126m)

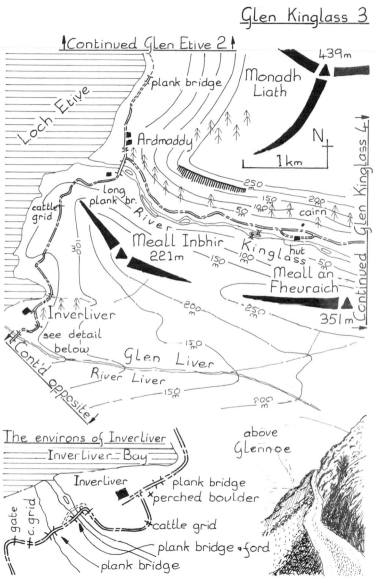

↑Continued Glen Etive 2↑

439m

Monadh Liath

plank bridge

Loch Etive

Ardmaddy

N

1 km

Continued Glen Kinglass 4→

250 m

cattle grid

long plank br.

River Kinglass

150   200

50   100

cairn

30/0

Meall Inbhir 221m

150

100

hut

50

Meall an Fheuraich

200

250

351m

Inverliver

see detail below

↓Cont'd opposite↓

Glen Liver

150

River Liver

150

200 m

The environs of Inverliver

Inverliver Bay

above Glennoe

Inverliver

plank bridge

perched boulder

gate

c. grid

cattle grid

plank bridge • ford

plank bridge

Glen Kinglass 4

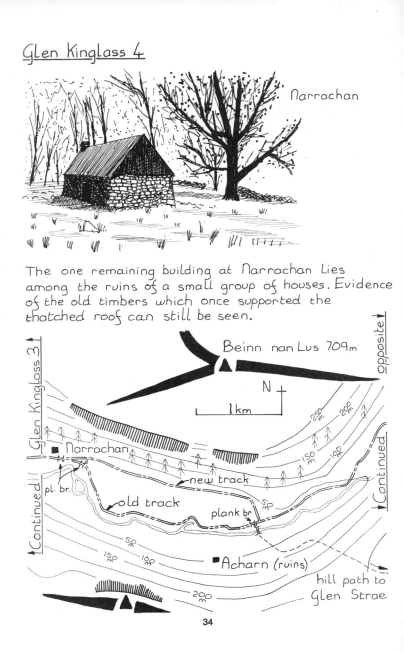

Narrachan

The one remaining building at Narrachan lies
among the ruins of a small group of houses. Evidence
of the old timbers which once supported the
thatched roof can still be seen.

opposite ►

Beinn nan Lus 709m

N

1 km

◄ Glen Kinglass 3

◄ Continued

Continued ►

Narrachan

250 m   200 m

150 m   100 m

new track

pl. br.

old track

plank br

50 m

50 m

150 m   100 m

Acharn (ruins)

200 m

hill path to
Glen Strae

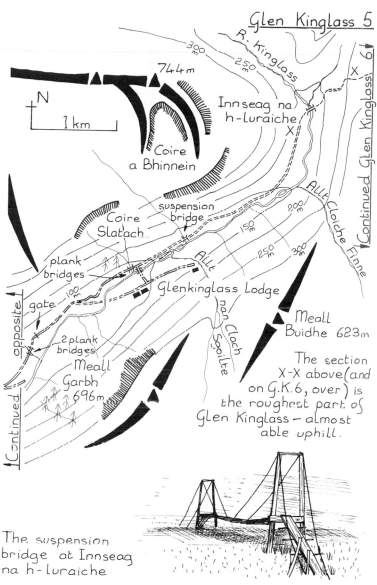

300m

250m

R. Kinglass

744m

Innseag na h-Luraiche

X

Continued Glen Kinglass 6

Coire a Bhinnein

suspension bridge

Coire Slatach

Allt Cloiche Finne

200m

150m

250m

300m

plank bridges

Allt

Glenkinglass Lodge

gate

100m

Allt nan Clach Spoilte

Meall Buidhe 623m

2 plank bridges

Meall Garbh 696m

Continued

opposite

The section X-X above (and on G.K.6, over) is the roughest part of Glen Kinglass - almost able uphill.

The suspension bridge at Innseag na h-Luraiche

35

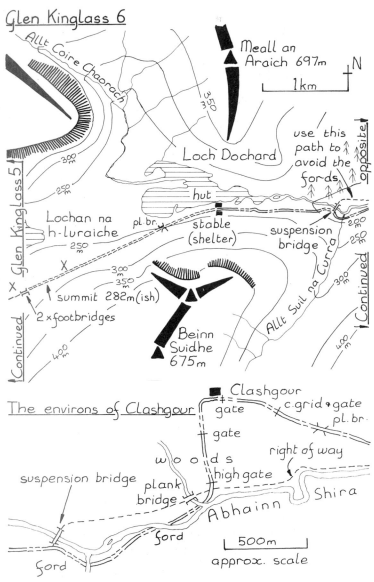

Glen Kinglass 6

Allt Coire Chaorach

Meall an Araich 697m

N

1km

Glen Kinglass 5

300 m
350 m
250 m

Loch Dochard

use this path to ↑↑ avoid the fords

opposite

hut

Lochan na h-luraiche

250 m

pl. br.

stable (shelter)

suspension bridge

200 m
250 m
300 m

X

summit 282m(ish)

300 m
350 m

Beinn Suidhe 675m

Allt Suil na Curra

Continued

Continued

400 m

2 × footbridges

400 m

The environs of Clashgour

Clashgour

gate

c. grid & gate
pl. br.

gate

right of way

w o o d s

high gate

suspension bridge

plank bridge

Shira

Abhainn

Ford

Ford

500m

approx. scale

36

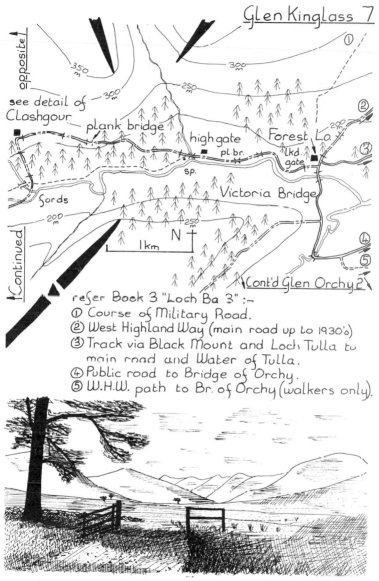

① 300 m

350 m

300 m

250 m

opposite ↑

see detail of Clashgour

plank bridge

high gate

Forest Lo.

②

pl. br.

lkd. gate

③

200 m

sp.

Sords

Victoria Bridge

200 m

250 m

N ↑

1 km

④

⑤

Continued ←

Cont'd Glen Orchy 2

refer Book 3 "Loch Ba 3":—

① Course of Military Road.
② West Highland Way (main road up to 1930's)
③ Track via Black Mount and Loch Tulla to main road and Water of Tulla.
④ Public road to Bridge of Orchy.
⑤ W.H.W. path to Br. of Orchy (walkers only).

37

Glen Orchy 1

The Glen Orchy track is unique in that your humble author, in all his research to date has never come across anything quite like it! It is an A.T.V. (all terrain vehicle) trail, smooth enough to be a ═══ but as steep in places as a ----. As a compromise I have graded it ════ .
This route lacks views so does not form a good walking path, and is hard to cycle. (Cyclists will be too busy to bother about the view!) It is very hard work if, like your author, you rode Glen Kinglass in the same day. As a "technical" bike ride it's just great!

1 km N

ford

esp.

oppo site

Allt Coire Bhiocair

lg. ford

A.T.V. trail

Continued

the only view point

A.T.V. trail

Allt Broighleachan

River Orchy

tree reserve

large ford

gate

B8074

Thanks should go to Forest Enterprise for being enterprising (sorry!) enough to provide something a bit different. The quiet Glen Orchy road provides a pleasant return trip - or alternative if Glen Kinglass was ridden in the morning.

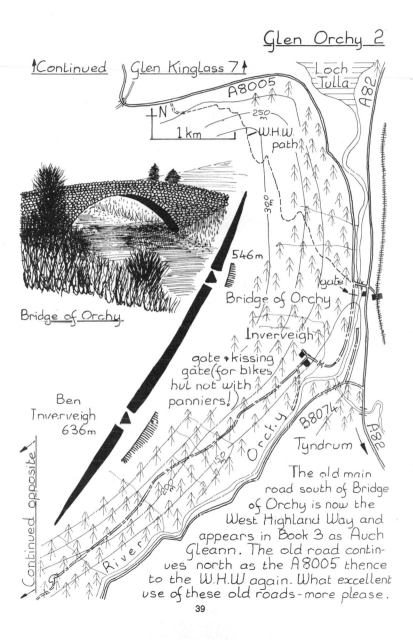

↑Continued   Glen Kinglass 7↑

Loch Tulla

A8005

A82

┼N

1 km

250 m

W.H.W. path

300 m

546m

Bridge of Orchy

gate

Bridge of Orchy.

Inverveigh

gate + kissing gate (for bikes but not with panniers!)

Ben Inverveigh 636m

River Orchy

B8074

Tyndrum

A82

Continued opposite

The old main road south of Bridge of Orchy is now the West Highland Way and appears in Book 3 as Auch Gleann. The old road continues north as the A8005 thence to the W.H.W again. What excellent use of these old roads - more please.

Glen Strae 1

Glen Strae provides the opportunity to explore a
wild and seemingly remote glen without much effort.
Once past the woods (and the cattle) the mood
of the glen changes to one of wilderness despite
being only 9km or 6miles from the road to the end
of the track. There is no
shelter in the glen.

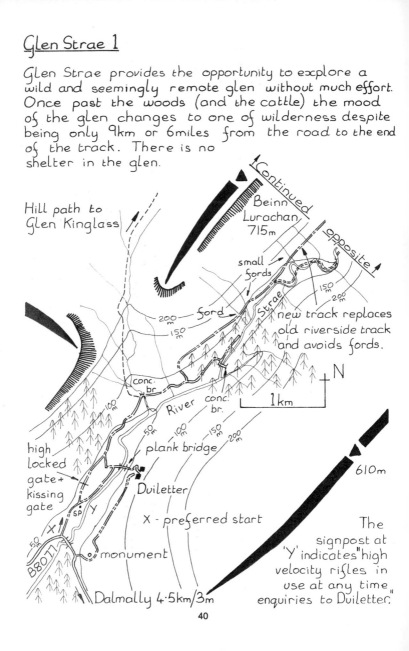

Continued opposite

Beinn
Lurachan
715m

Hill path to
Glen Kinglass

small
fords

ford

Strae

new track replaces
old riverside track
and avoids fords.

200
m
150
m

N

1km

conc.
br.

River   conc.
br.

100
m
50
m
100
m
150
m
200
m

610m

high
locked
gate +
kissing
gate

plank bridge

Duiletter

SP   Y

X

X - preferred start

B8077

monument

The
signpost at
'Y' indicates "high
velocity rifles in
use at any time,
enquiries to Duiletter."

Dalmally 4·5km/3m

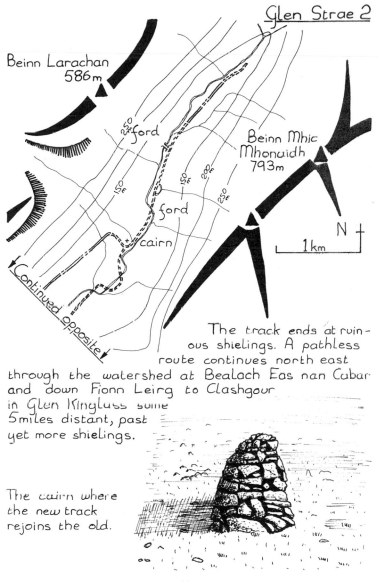

Glen Strae 2

Beinn Larachan
586m

ford

ford

cairn

Beinn Mhic
Mhonuidh
793m

N

1 km

Continued opposite

The track ends at ruin-
ous shielings. A pathless
route continues north east
through the watershed at Bealach Eas nan Cubar
and down Fionn Leirg to Clashgour
in Glen Kinglass some
5 miles distant, past
yet more shielings.

The cairn where
the new track
rejoins the old.

41

Oban to Inveraray

Oban to Inveraray

Access:- This section includes Loch Awe and land bounded by:- the Pass of Brander to Oban road; the coast south to Lochgilphead; Loch Fyne and the Inveraray to Dalmally road. Connections with the rest of civilisation are east to Tyndrum, via Glen Lochy, and over the Rest and be Thankful pass to Loch Lomond. The only railway runs across the north of the region from Tyndrum to Oban. A few delightful minor roads run into the heart of the region and around Loch Awe.

Accommodation:- Oban, Lochgilphead and Inveraray are the main centres, all with the usual info' centres. (L'gilph'd March to October opening). Oban and Inverary boast SYHA hostels. Campsites are thinly spread away from the main tourist centres.

Geographical Features:- Be quick!... this area is fast disappearing under a blanket of trees. Whilst your author likes forests - and the resultant tracks provide good walking and cycling- the phrase "enough is enough" springs to mind when considering the extent of commercial planting..... Unlike Lorn to the north, here we have fresh water lochs and low hills which define themselves into rocky south west/ north east ridges around their low summits. A complete contrast with the previous section, Lorn. (Yes, I know Lorn extends into the north of this section, hence String of Lorn, but my boundaries/regions are somewhat arbitrary!)

Mountains:- None! 'Knobbly lumps' may better describe the topography. The proper mountains sadly give up at Ben Cruachan to the north and around the head of Glen Shira to the east. The highest point in the region is Cruach Mhor between Loch Awe and Tullich and that's only

589m, not even 2000ft. never mind 3000! Sorry, you can't have everything!

Rivers:- The drainage into, and out of Loch Awe is a little odd as it looks at first glance as if its outlet is at Ford, the south west end. However the Orchy and the Awe both feed and drain the north end. The position of Loch Awe means all rivers in the region are short, possibly the R. Add being the most interesting, though much of this is borrowed for Loch Glashan. The high rainfall of the region ensures that these short rivers can become raging torrents in their journey to the sea (or Loch Awe).

Forests:- Kilmichael, Inverliever and Eredine are the largest in a region heading towards becoming one giant-sized forest. I must mention here two omissions from the routes I could have included. One is Fearnoch Forest between Loch Etive and Glen Lonan. The routes are too short for my preference and parking is difficult at entries to the forest. However, Forest Enterprise have marked trails for bikes. The second fairly obvious omission is Raera Forest between Loch Melfort and Loch Feochan. This forest is devoid of any interest. The tracks lead one round and round a seemingly abandoned forest (at the time of my survey) with no views, nowhere to stop (other than to sit on the track), and no points of interest. Much as I like cycling I was bored witless in Raera Forest!

Lochs:- Loch Awe dominates but Lochs Avich and Scammadale have their quiet charm. Loch Nant was half full and ugly but is probably quite scenic when full to the brim.

Emergency:- Civilisation is nearly always near at hand, the only exception being around Carron (Eredine Forest to Ford/L. Glashan) which is a bit remote - so care needed in severe weather.

Oban to Inveraray Routes 1

Loch Nant

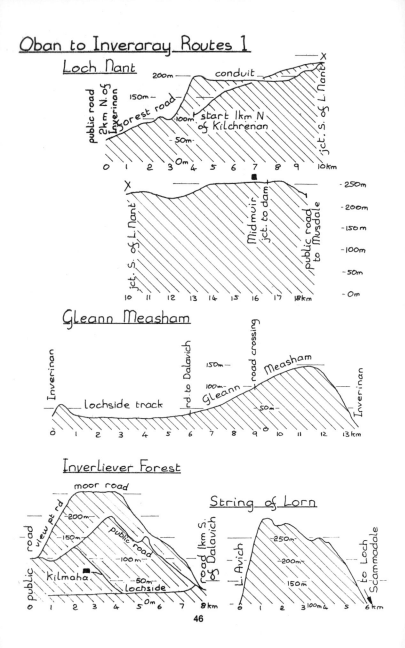

Gleann Measham

Inverliever Forest

String of Lorn

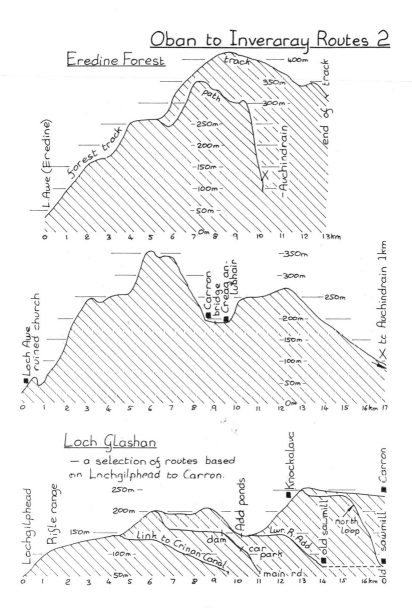

Eredine Forest

track — 400m
350m
path
300m
end of track
250m
200m
Auchindrain
150m
100m
50m
0m

L.Awe (Eredine)
forest track

0 1 2 3 4 5 6 7 8 9 10 11 12 13km

—350m
—300m
250m
Carron bridge
Creag an Lubhair
200m
to Auchindrain 1km
150m
100m
50m
0m

Loch Awe
ruined church

0 1 2 3 4 5 6 7 8 9 10 11 12 13 14 15 16km 17

Loch Glashan

— a selection of routes based on Lochgilphead to Carron.

250m —

Lochgilphead
Rifle range
200m
Add ponds
Knockalava
Carron
150m
Link to Crinan Canal
dam
Lwr. R. Add
old sawmill
north Loop
sawmill
100m
car park
main rd.
old sawmill
50m

0 1 2 3 4 5 6 7 8 9 10 11 12 13 14 15 16km 0

47

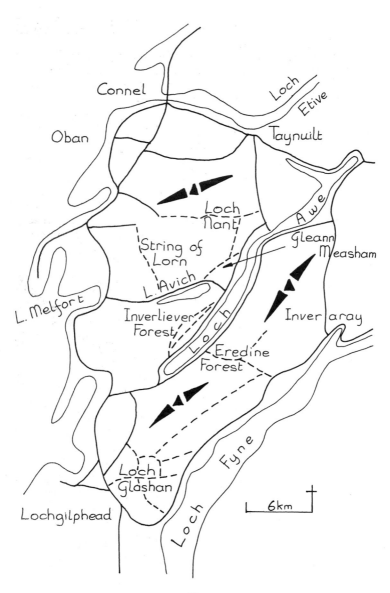

Connel

Loch Etive

Oban

Taynuilt

Loch Nant

Awe

Gleann Measham

String of Lorn

L. Avich

L. Melfort

Inverliever Forest

Loch

Inveraray

Eredine Forest

Loch Fyne

Loch Glashan

Lochgilphead

6km

48

The Loch Nant tracks link the minor Glen Feochan road, from Oban, to Kilchrenan on Loch Awe and the Gleann Measham tracks. Together with the String of Lorn these almost provide a circular tour from Oban. That said, the environs of Loch Nant are worthy of exploration in their own right, and this is best done from Loch Awe, starting as indicated on Loch Nant 3, continuing to the dam*(below) and/or Glen Feochan public road and returning to Kilchrenan (just north of). There is no shelter but there is the rare luxury of a picnic table! See distance map over for Loch Nant and its links to the above routes and Oban. Due to the extensive metalled sections of road Loch Nant is more suited to cycling than walking.

to Oban

360 m

Creag Mhor

dam

250 m

300 m

250 m

gate

241 m

S.P. "Public footpath to Kilchrenan"

plank bridges

Gleann Fearna

Midmuir (ruins)

public road

Loch Nant 2

Continued

200 m

Musdale

N

1km

dam*

Beinn Dearg

482 m

300 m

350 m

300 m

350 m

250 m

150 m

200 m

250 m

300 m

150 m

400 m

300 m

Loch Nant 2

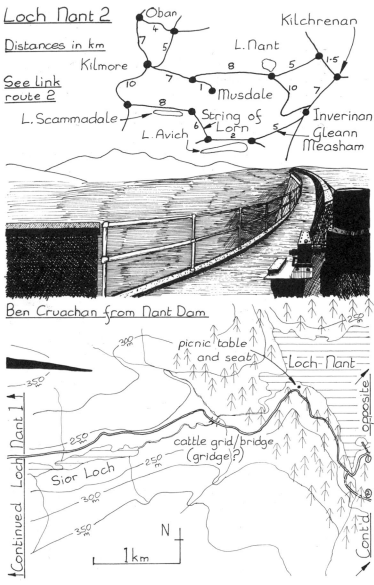

Distances in km

See link
route 2

Oban

Kilchrenan

L. Nant

Kilmore

7
4
5
7
8
5
1·5

10
1
Musdale
10
7

L. Scammadale
8
String of Lorn
6
L. Avich
2
5
Inverinan
Gleann Measham

Ben Cruachan from Nant Dam

Continued Loch Nant 1

300m
350m
250m

picnic table and seat

Loch Nant

250m
cattle grid/bridge (gridge?)
250m

Sior Loch
300m
350m

opposite

Cont'd

N

1 km

The footpaths converging on 'Y' are
falling into disuse due to the construction
of the Loch Nant dam road. This
right-of-way, X-X, will be
lost to undergrowth
and trees if it is
not used.

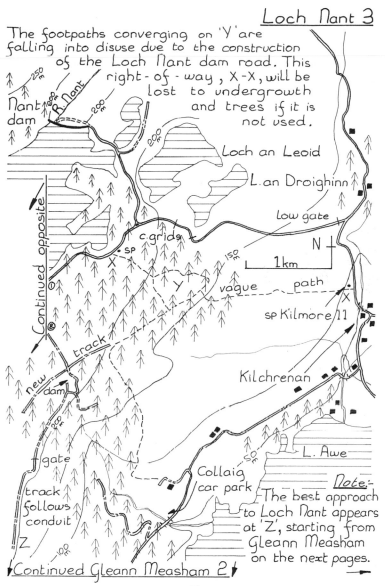

R. Nant

Nant
dam

250ᵐ
200ᵐ
200ᵐ
200ᵐ

Loch an Leoid

L. an Droighinn

low gate

N

1km

Continued opposite

c.grids

• SP

X

①

Y   vague   path   •X

150ᵐ

sp Kilmore 11

②

track

new
dam

200ᵐ

Kilchrenan

gate

track
follows
conduit

Z

00ᵐ

Collaig
car park

50ᵐ

L. Awe

<u>Note</u>:-
The best approach
to Loch Nant appears
at 'Z', starting from
Gleann Measham
on the next pages.

<u>Continued Gleann Measham 2</u>

Gleann Measham 1

The tracks based on Gleann Measham provide a variety of scenery; river, waterfalls, forest and lochside, all with little effort. A pleasant circuit of 14km or 9miles is easily accomplished from either Inverinan or Dalavich. Note the tracks on the opposite page which form the link to, and indeed provide the best starting point for Loch Nant. The proximity of the String of Lorn track is shown below as part of the circular tour set out on Loch Nant 2 and in more detail as "Link Route 2" in the final section of this guide.

N

1 km
300 m

365m
▲ Créag nan Cuilean

250 m

200 m

vague path

vague path

Gleann Measham

150 m

Cont'd String of Lorn

gates

150 m

Kilmelford

100 m

concrete bridge

gates

250 m

200 m

303m ▲

views

Loch Avich

forest walk

100 m

Avich Falls

150 m

Continued Inverliever Forest 2

① ② ③ ④ ⑤ ⑥ ⑦

opposite

Continued

gate

52

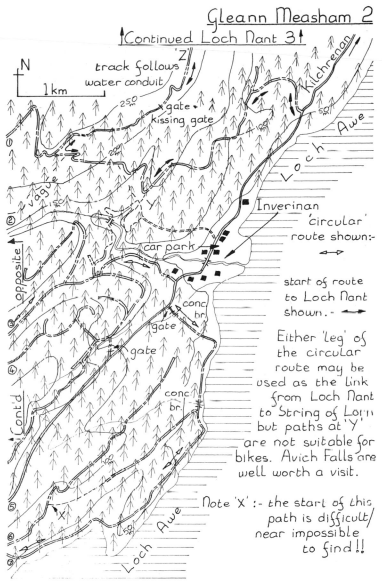

N

1 km

track follows
water conduit

'Z'

gate
kissing gate

Kilchrenan

Loch Awe

vague

'Y'

car park

Inverinan

'circular'
route shown:-

↔

start of route
to Loch Nant
shown. - ↔

opposite

conc
br.

gate

gate

conc.
br.

Either 'leg' of
the circular
route may be
used as the link
from Loch Nant
to String of Lorn
but paths at 'Y'
are not suitable for
bikes. Avich Falls are
well worth a visit.

Note 'X' :- the start of this
        path is difficult/
        near impossible
        to find!!

'X'

Loch Awe

Cont'd

Inverliever Forest 1

Inverliever Forest lies to the north west of the upper reaches of Loch Awe. Its tracks provide both lochside and hill forest tracks, divided by the public road and of a variety not depicted on the O.S. maps. Indeed, apart from the mixed woodland of the loch shore there is about a square km of ancient oakwood west of Dalavich, the subject of a very pleasant forest walk, yet the O.S. doggedly insist all is conifer plantation. Perhaps someone should tell them! There is no shelter but a considerable mileage of tracks is available within close proximity to the car parks allowing a rapid return to base if required.

N

1km

Continued opposite

Barmaddy Road

gate

Moor Road

Middle Road

D

concrete bridge

parking

Tower Road

C

Dun Carroch Road

Awe

B

View Point Rd.

park + picnic

conc. br.

A

Loch

park + picnic

A maze of dead-ends frustrate the unwary. Road connections at A, B, C, etc. indicate the starting points for usable routes into the forest. The public road is very hilly—be warned.

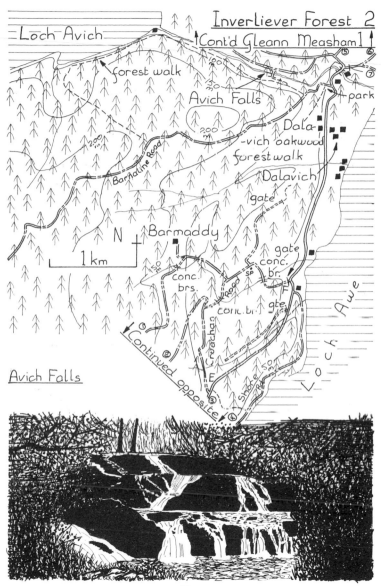

Loch Avich

Cont'd Gleann Measham 1

forest walk

Avich Falls

Dala-
-vich oakwood
forest walk

Dalavich

park

gate

Barmaddy

gate
conc.
br.

N

1 km

conc.
brs.

conc. br.

Barnaline Road

gate

F

gte.

Loch Awe

Croachan

Shore Rd

Continued opposite

E

Avich Falls

55

String of Lorn

The String of Lorn Road forms an important link between Loch Avich and Loch Scammadale as shown in Link Route 2 in the final section of this book.

Despite the steep and unrelenting climb from Loch Avich, this is the best end to start for a bike as the path section is then negotiated down hill. Total distance is only 6km, 4 miles, between public roads.

to Loch Scammadale

fords

Note:- half way along Loch Scammadale the String of Lorn right-of-way continues north to Kilmore.

Fineglen

indistinct path crosses the burn just below a waterfall.

N

1km

Loch na Sreinge

fords gate & stile

gates

forest track runs to dead-ends

373m

Cruach Narrachan

high gate

low gate

to Kilmelford

Continued Gleann Measham 1

56

Eredine Forest offers a variety of possibilities:-
Firstly, the steep forest track climbs out of Eredine
by Loch Awe heading south east, then turning to
head north east on a fine high level traverse
with views over Douglas Water. Regrettably this
track runs to a dead end but its exploration is still
worthwhile. Secondly, a wet walkers' path heads
from the top of the climb to Auchindrain, by the
folk museum on the Inveraray to Loch Fyne road.
Thirdly, a further track climbs from Auchindrain
and runs to Carron where this divides; a) to follow
a vague path which forms a tenuous link to the
Loch Glashan tracks and b) a hill path to the
southern tip of Loch Awe making possible a fine
'circular' route. The only shelter is in the
bothy at Carron, and the shed at the top of the
climb from Eredine. The stone bridge just before
Carron indicates the past importance of these old
tracks. This bridge is omitted from the O.S. map.
Map pages are
as below:-

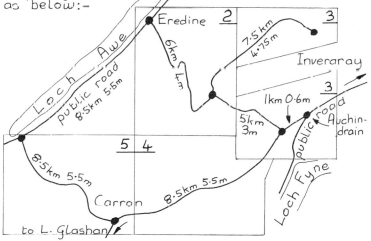

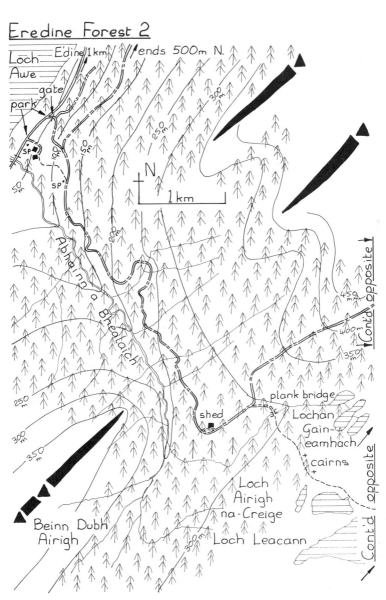

Eredine Forest 2

Loch Awe

Edine 1km

ends 500m N.

gate

park

sp

sp

Abhainn a Bhealaich

N

1km

250m

300m

200m

150m

50m

450m

400m

350m

plank bridge

shed

Lochan Gain-eamhach

cairns

250m

300m

350m

Loch Airigh na-Creige

Loch Leacann

Beinn Dubh Airigh

300m

Cont'd opposite

Cont'd opposite

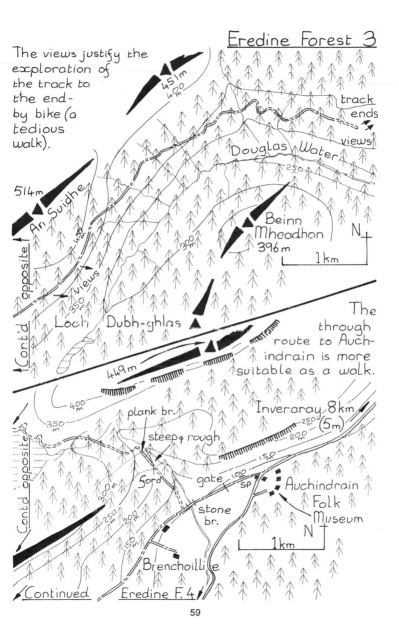

The views justify the exploration of the track to the end—by bike (a tedious walk).

track ends

views

451m
400m

Douglas Water

250

514m

An Suidhe

Beinn Mheadhon
396m

N

1 km

Cont'd opposite

300m

350m

views

Loch Dubh-ghlas

The through route to Auchindrain is more suitable as a walk.

449m

400m

350m

Inveraray 8km
(5m)

250m
200m

plank br.

steep & rough

150

gate
100
SP

Auchindrain
Folk Museum

Sord

N

1 km

300m

250m
200m

stone br.

Cont'd opposite

150m

Brenchoillie

Continued   Eredine F. 4

Eredine Forest 4

↑Continued Eredine Forest 3↑

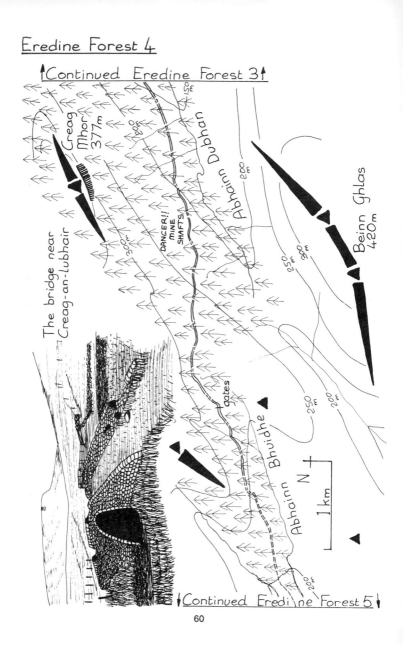

Creag Mhor 377m

The bridge near Creag-an-lubhair

DANGER!! MINE SHAFTS

Abhainn Dubhan

Beinn Ghlas 420m

gates

Abhainn Bhuidhe

N

1 km

↓Continued Eredine Forest 5↓

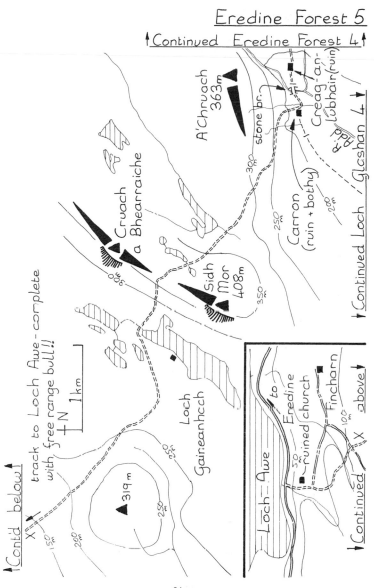

↑Contid below↑

X

track to Loch Awe - complete
with free range bull!!

↓N
├─ 1km ─┤

319 m

Loch Gaineanhcch

A'Chruach 363m

stone br.

Cruach a Bhearraiche

Sidh Mor 408m

Carron (ruin + bothy)

Creag-an-Lùbhair (ruin)

R.R.pt.

to Eredine

Loch-Awe

ruined church

Fincharn

X

↓Continued

↑above↑

↓Continued Loch / Gleshan 4

61

Loch Glashan 1

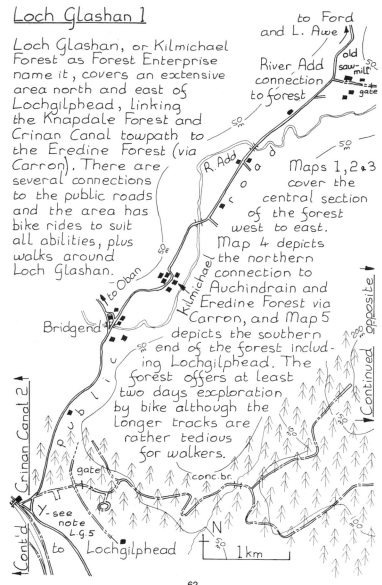

Loch Glashan, or Kilmichael Forest as Forest Enterprise name it, covers an extensive area north and east of Lochgilphead, linking the Knapdale Forest and Crinan Canal towpath to the Eredine Forest (via Carron). There are several connections to the public roads and the area has bike rides to suit all abilities, plus walks around Loch Glashan.

to Ford and L. Awe

River Add connection to forest

old saw-mill

gate

R. Add

Maps 1, 2 & 3 cover the central section of the forest west to east. Map 4 depicts the northern connection to Auchindrain and Eredine Forest via Carron, and Map 5 depicts the southern end of the forest including Lochgilphead. The forest offers at least two days exploration by bike although the longer tracks are rather tedious for walkers.

to Oban

Kilmichael

Bridgend

Continued opposite

Public

Crinan Canal 2

Cont'd

gate

Y - see note L.G.5

conc. br.

N

to Lochgilphead

1 km

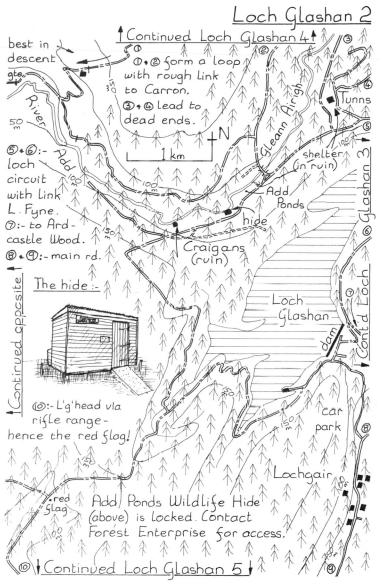

↑Continued Loch Glashan 4↑

① • ② form a loop
with rough Link
to Carron.
③ • ④ lead to
dead ends.

⑤ • ⑥:-
loch
circuit
with Link
L. Fyne.
⑦:- to Ard-
castle Wood.
⑧ • ⑨:- main rd.

best in descent
gte.

River Add

50 m

Gleann Airigh

Tunns

shelter
(in ruin)

Add
Ponds

hide

Craigans
(ruin)

100 m

150 m

1 km

N

The hide :-

⑩:- L'g'head via
rifle range -
hence the red flag!

Loch
Glashan

dam

car
park

Lochgair

red
flag

Add Ponds Wildlife Hide
(above) is locked. Contact
Forest Enterprise for access.

Cont'd Loch

← Continued opposite

↓ Continued Loch Glashan 5 ↓

Blackmill Loch

N

1km

▲ 276m ▲ 271m

A83

to Inveraray

conc. brs.

④ ⑤

Glashan 2

⑥

Loch

⑦

Cont'd

A83

⑧

Cnoc nam Broighleag 314m

200m

150m

100m

gte

gate park

Ardcastle ꓔ Wood

gte

Loch Gair

Loch Fyne

The tracks and paths of Ardcastle Wood form a separate excursion - better suited to walkers due to the limited length of the tracks and number of '----' paths. Forest Enterprise sensibly discourage the joint use of '---' paths by both walkers & bikes.

Knockalava, above, lies as evidence that these ruins were once home and livelihood to those hardy folk who farmed the high glens. Creag an Iubhair, Carron, Lower Carron, Knockalava, Tunns and Craigans; Six farms engulfed by trees and "progress".

This map depicts the tenuous connection to Carron, and the top end of the loop track north of Loch Glashan, best anti-clockwise. There is shelter at Knockalava (and Tunns) but obviously care is needed around these ruinous buildings.

Carron

Continued Ericadine Forest 5

1km

River Add

Airigh

Knockalava

Airigh Ard 226m

N

|___1km___|

250 m

gate

Glesarn

① ↓Cont'd Loch Glashan ② 2↓ ③

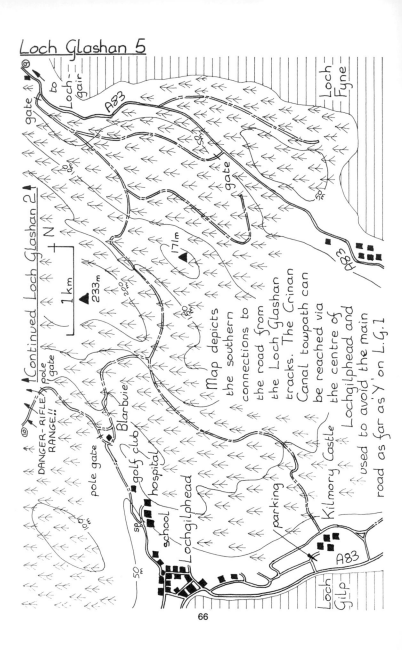

to Loch-gair

Loch Fyne

gate

A83

A83

gate

Continued Loch Glashan 2

N

1 km

233m

171m

pole gate

DANGER- RIFLE RANGE!!

pole gate

Blarbuie

golf club

hospital

school

Lochgilphead

parking

Kilmory Castle

A83

Loch Gilp

Map depicts the southern connections to the road from the Loch Glashan tracks. The Crinan Canal towpath can be reached via the centre of Lochgilphead and used to avoid the main road as far as 'Y' on L.G.1

66

East of Loch Awe and Cowal

East of Loch Awe and Cowal

Access:- This extensive area lies south of the Crianlarich to Dalmally road and, bordered by Glen Aray in the west and Loch Lomond in the east, continues south to the Kyles of Bute. Access from main centres is via Tarbet, straight into Ardgartan from which several routes radiate, and most others are within striking distance. The Dunoon ferries provide a useful short-cut into Cowal from south of the Clyde.

Accommodation:- There is a tourist information centre at Tarbet on Loch Lomond (Apr-Oct) and another in Dunoon. Ardgartan is well served with camping and caravan sites as is the route north to Tyndrum. Dunoon offers a variety of accommodation but this once fine resort is a mere shadow of its former Victorian grandeur, once popular with the steamer trips from Glasgow. Now folk no longer go "doon the water" (yet another tradition destroyed by the motor car), and with the closure of the U.S. base at Holy Loch, Dunoon was visibly struggling to survive when visited by your author. I digress! A thin sprinkling of B.Bs is to be found throughout the area, and a hotel or two in most small towns. There are SYHA hostels at Ardgartan and Tighnabruaich.

Geographical Features:- The area has many fine mountains to the north and these diminish in height as one travels south, where the glens deepen to form sea lochs, fjord-like in character, around the Cowal peninsula. The northern glens provide the wildest routes in this guide book, contrasting with forest and lochside to the south.

Mountains:- Many fine mountains stand proudly to the north of the region. These are individual summits, not connected by obvious ridges, each with its own character. Ben Lui, Ben Oss, Ben Ime and Ben Vorlich are probably the best known Munros whilst the lesser Ben Arthur (The Cobbler) relies upon its dramatic profile for its fame. The northern glens form the approach routes to these hills. The rounded hills to the south lack both height and interest by comparison.

Rivers:- In such a complex peninsula rivers are short, the River Fyne and River Shira in the north being the longest. The high Argyll rainfall, however, ensures that despite their lack of miles the lower reaches of these can become raging torrents, far too dangerous to cross safely. There are however no serious river crossings on the routes described, bridges being provided at all strategic locations.

Forests:- Cowal is fast disappearing under a blanket of trees. I am tempted to say "enough is enough", even though afforestation provides most of the routes on the following pages. If all is forest these routes become less attractive. Fortunately both the wilder glens in the north and picturesque lochsides provide a break in the trees-until still more is planted....

Lochs:- Loch Eck, the only sizeable natural loch is a gem. The only other large stretches of fresh water are Loch Sloy and Lochan Shira - complete with huge dams. Sea lochs abound; Loch Fyne, Kyles of Bute, Loch Striven, Holy Loch, Loch Long and Loch Goil. Loch Lomond borders this region but this belongs to the neighbouring book covering The Trossachs.

Emergency:- All routes lie near habitation except for the walk/cycle linking Glens Fyne and Shira and the through walks to the north which are quite committing requiring good weather and care.

East of Loch Awe and Cowal Routes 1

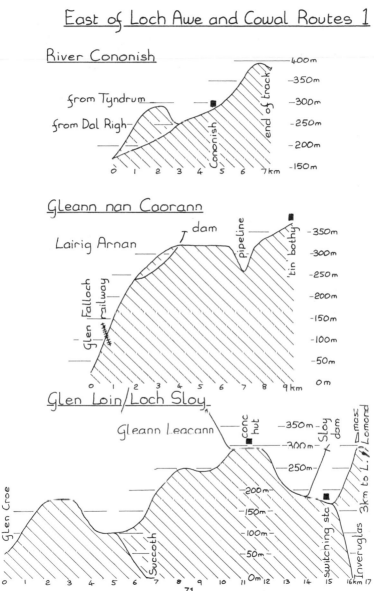

River Cononish

- 400m
- 350m

from Tyndrum — 300m

from Dal Righ — 250m

- 200m

Cononish | end of track — 150m

0 1 2 3 4 5 6 7km

Gleann nan Caorann

dam

Lairig Arnan

pipeline 'tin' bothy — 350m
- 300m

Glen Falloch railway — 250m
- 200m
- 150m
- 100m
- 50m

0 1 2 3 4 5 6 7 8 9km   0m

Glen Loin/Loch Sloy

Gleann Leacann   conc hut — 350m

Sloy dam — 300m

moss to L. Lomond — 250m
- 200m

Glen Croe   switching sta — 150m
- 100m

Succoth — 50m

Inveruglas   3km to L. Lomond — 0m

0 1 2 3 4 5 6 7 8 9 10 11 12 13 14 15 16km 17

East of Loch Awe and Cowal Routes 2

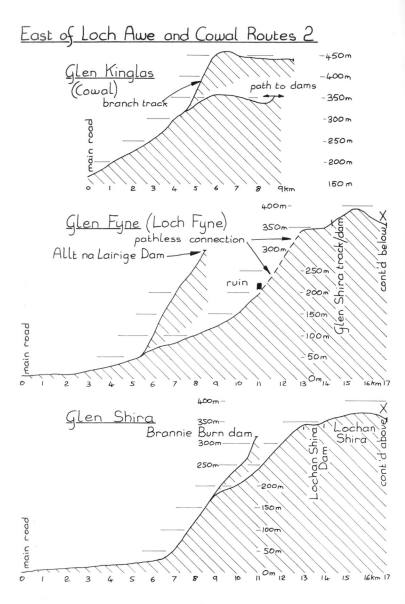

Glen Kinglas (Cowal)

branch track

path to dams

- 450 m
- 400 m
- 350 m
- 300 m
- 250 m
- 200 m
- 150 m

main road

0 1 2 3 4 5 6 7 8 9 km

Glen Fyne (Loch Fyne)

pathless connection

Allt na Lairige Dam

ruin

Glen Shira track/dam

cont'd below X

400 m
350 m
300 m
250 m
200 m
150 m
100 m
50 m
0 m

main road

0 1 2 3 4 5 6 7 8 9 10 11 12 13 14 15 16 km 17

Glen Shira

Brannie Burn dam

Lochan Shira Dam

Lochan Shira

cont'd above X

400 m
350 m
300 m
250 m
200 m
150 m
100 m
50 m
0 m

main road

0 1 2 3 4 5 6 7 8 9 10 11 12 13 14 15 16 km 17

72

East of Loch Awe and Cowal Routes 3

Ardgartan Forest

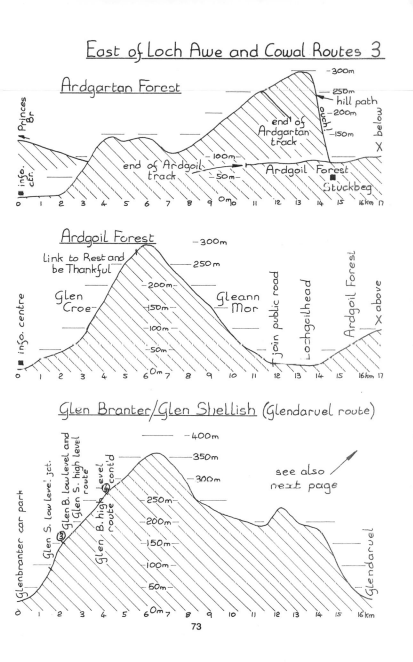

Ardgoil Forest

Glen Branter/Glen Shellish (Glendaruel route)

see also
next page

East of Loch Awe and Cowal Routes 4

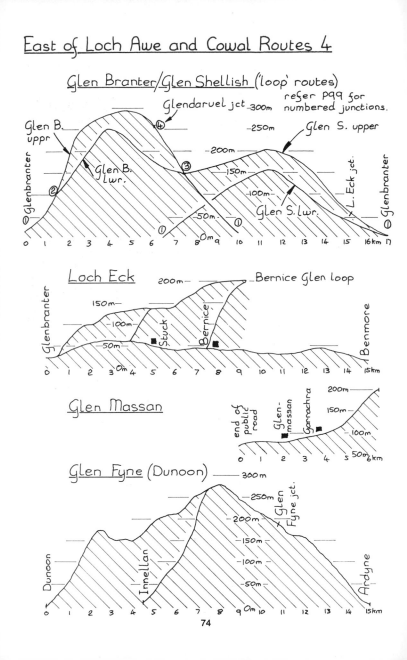

Glen Branter/Glen Shellish ('loop' routes)

refer P99 for numbered junctions.

Glendaruel jct

Glen B. uppr

Glen B. Lwr.

Glen S. upper

Glen S. Lwr.

L. Eck jct.

Glenbranter

Glenbranter

Glenbranter

Loch Eck

Bernice Glen loop

Glenbranter

Stuck

Bernice

Benmore

Glen Massan

end of public road

Glen-massan

Garrachra

Glen Fyne (Dunoon)

Dunoon

Innellan

Glen Fyne jct.

Ardyne

74

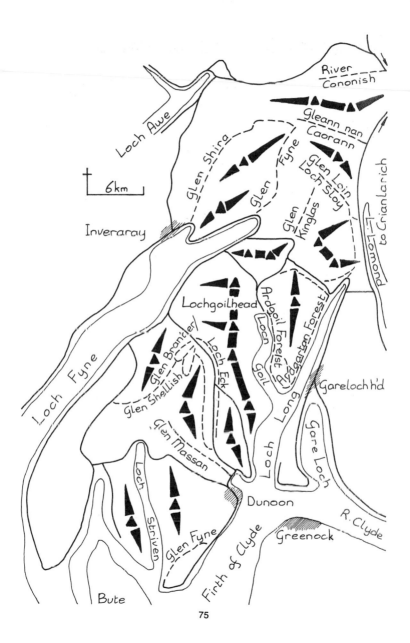

River Cononish

Loch Awe

Gleann nan Caorann

Glen Shira

Glen Fyne

Glen Loin
Loch Sloy

6km

Glen Kinglas

to Crianlarich

Inveraray

Loch Lomond

Lochgoilhead

Ardgoil Forest

Loch Goil

Ardgartan Forest

Loch Fyne

Glen Branter

Loch Eck

Glen Shellish

Loch Long

Gareloch'd

Glen Massan

Gare Loch

Loch Striven

Glen Fyne

Dunoon

R. Clyde

Greenock

Bute

Firth of Clyde

75

River Cononish 1

The River Cononish track, just south of Tyndrum is the hillwalkers' and climbers' approach to Ben Lui and Ben Oss (if only all Munros had such simple names!) The track is totally dominated by the presence of Ben Lui, a beautiful mountain standing proudly at the head of this nameless glen. The end of the track is a short 7km (4.5 miles) from the main road and a similar distance from Tyndrum.

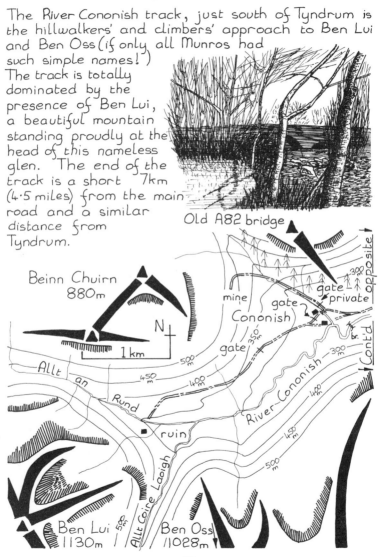

Old A82 bridge

Beinn Chuirn 880m

N

1 km

Allt an Rund

ruin

mine

Cononish

gate private

gate

gate

br.

River Cononish

Contd opposite

Allt Coire Laoigh

Ben Lui 1130m

Ben Oss 1028m

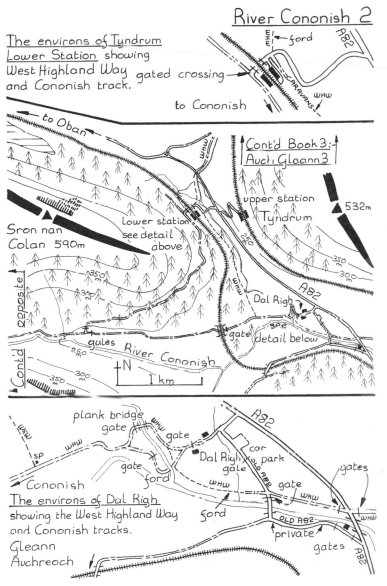

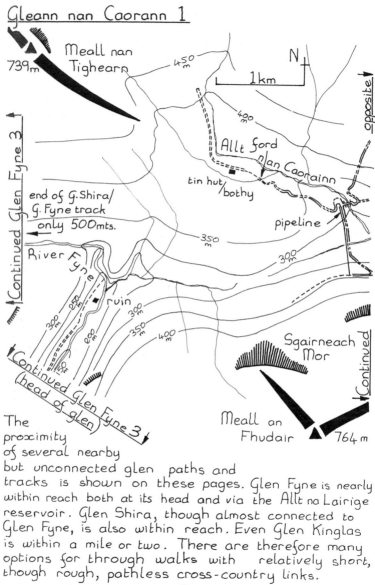

The
proximity
of several nearby
but unconnected glen paths and
tracks is shown on these pages. Glen Fyne is nearly
within reach both at its head and via the Allt na Lairige
reservoir. Glen Shira, though almost connected to
Glen Fyne, is also within reach. Even Glen Kinglas
is within a mile or two. There are therefore many
options for through walks with relatively short,
though rough, pathless cross-country links.

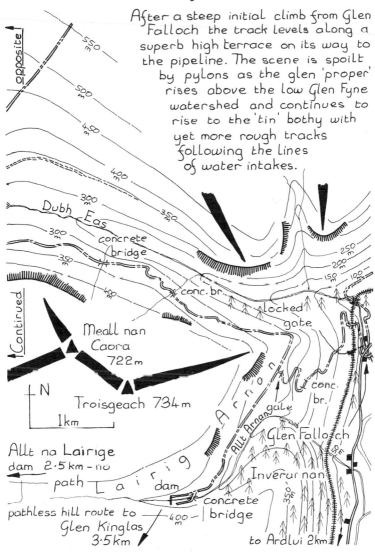

Gleann nan Caorann 2

After a steep initial climb from Glen Falloch the track levels along a superb high terrace on its way to the pipeline. The scene is spoilt by pylons as the glen 'proper' rises above the low Glen Fyne watershed and continues to rise to the 'tin' bothy with yet more rough tracks following the lines of water intakes.

opposite

550 m
500 m
450 m
400 m

Dubh Eas
300 m
300 m
350 m
concrete bridge
350 m
400 m
250 m
200 m
150 m
100 m

conc. br.

locked gate

Continued

Meall nan Caora 722m

N

Troisgeach 734m

1km

conc. br.

gate

Glen Falloch

Allt na Lairige
dam 2.5km - no
path

Inverurnan

Allt Arnan

L a i r i g e
dam

pathless hill route to
Glen Kinglas
3.5km

400 m
concrete bridge

350 m

to Ardlui 2km

79

Glen Loin/Loch Sloy 1

The tracks of Glen Loin and Loch Sloy give hillwalkers access to some distinguished mountains; Ben Vorlich, Ben Vane, Ben Ime, Beinn Narnain and The Cobbler all lie within reach of the following tracks. For cyclists the following pages should be carefully studied when planning sorties in this area as the main roads are very busy, ruling out a safe return by road. This is a disadvantage considering the widespread road connections:- Glen Croe; north of Arrochar at Succoth; Inveruglas (dam road); and Ardvorlich. Your author recommends an out-and-back run from Glen Croe to the mast above Loch Lomond. This provides a reasonable 16km (10m) each way increased by 5km (3m) by the return trip to the dam. The Loch Sloy roads are metalled and the descent to Ardvorlich is rough and inhabited by cattle. There is shelter -just- a miserable damp concrete hut in Gleann Leacann Sheileach. Standing in the pouring rain is preferable to this!

Cont'd Ardgoil 3

old road

N

1 km

park/start for Glen Loin

gate   old road   gate & stile

The Glen Croe connection belongs to Ardgartan Forest but it is more logical to use the main road as the division between routes.

main road

thro' track
dead end

Continued opposite

A83

↓Continued Ardgartan Forest 2↓

meagre shelter -
Gleann Leacann
Sheileach.

↑ Continued Glen Loin / Loch Sloy 3 ↑

← Ben Narnain

N

1 km

← Ben Narnain

Glen Loin

Cruach
Tairbeirt
415m

250m

150m

150m

200m

two concrete
bridges

concrete
bridge

Succoth

100m

150m

50m

Arrochar

Turbet

Lo-

Loch

Long

to Garelochhead

Your
author
would
never
encourage
his readers
to engage
upon such
dangerous
exploits as
exploring tunnels
Nor would he expect
the adventurous to
refrain from such
foolhardiness !! ....
- care!

← Continued opposite

Glen Loin/Loch Sloy 3

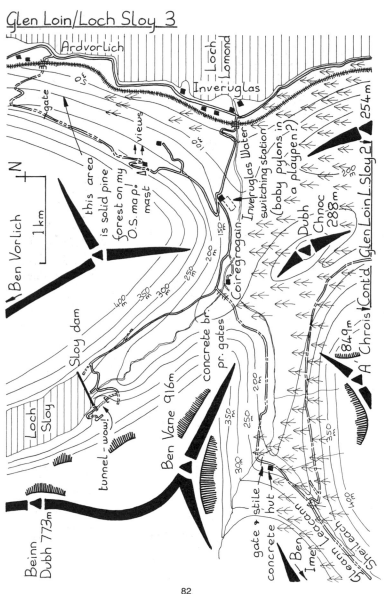

Ardvorlich

Loch Lomond

Inveruglas

O S

gate

views

O S

100

this area is solid pine forest on my O.S. map

mast

N

1 km

Ben Vorlich

Sloy dam

200 m

250 m

300 m

350 m

400 m

150 m

Coiregrogain

Inveruglas Water

switching station

(baby pylons in a playpen?)

254 m

300

Dubh Chnoc 288 m

Loch Sloy

tunnel - wow!

concrete br.

pr. gates

200 m

Ben Vane 916 m

350 m

250 m

A' Chrois

849 m

Cont'd Glen Loin L.Sloy 2

350 m

Beinn Dubh 773 m

300 m

gate + stile

concrete hut

Gleann na Leacann

Sgilleach

400

Ben Ime

100

Not to be confused with Glen Kinglass , Glen Kinglas is the poor relation. The track leaves the main road and one is immediately into a wild looking glen. However, the purpose of the track is soon clear; forestry , a sea of pylons, and intakes for the Loch Sloy hydro scheme. There is no shelter — yours truly got a thorough soaking in Glen Kinglas!

450 m

500 m

500 m

high gate

Continued opposite

Meall Beag
607m

high gates

low gate

597m

350

low gate

pathless descent to Glen Fyne, follow pylons — precipitous gorge Black Linn and Eagle's Fall lies to the north. Under 2km (1·2m) to walk.

748 m

500 m

450 m

350 m

Abysinnia (ruin)

dam

817 m

400 m

300 m

550 m

250 m

350 m

450 m

Inveraray/ Dunoon etc.

A83

250 m

400 m

450 m

N

1 km

park old road bridge

Rest and be Thankful road

Beinn Chorranach 885m

Ben Ime

Glen Kinglas 2

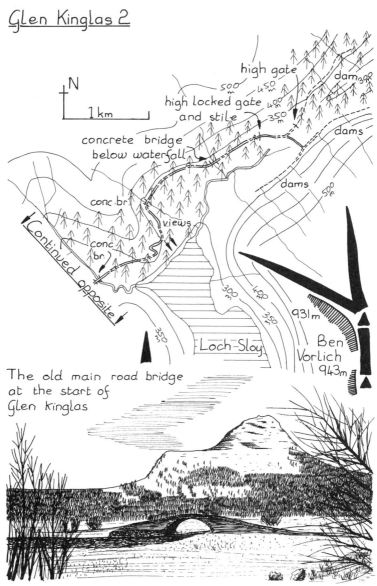

N

1 km

high gate

dam

high locked gate
and stile

500 m
450 m
400 m
350 m

dams

concrete bridge
below waterfall

dams

conc. br.

views

500 m

conc. br.

Continued opposite

300

400

350

931m

Loch Sloy

Ben
Vorlich
943m

350

The old main road bridge
at the start of
Glen Kinglas

Glen Fyne and its River Fyne drain into the head of Loch Fyne. The 'track' is a metalled road as far as Allt na Lairige dam. Interest is heightened as the glen track branches off and heads up the narrowing glen, eventually ending at a ruin within a mile of the end of the Glen Shira track which drops into the head of Glen Fyne. These two glens may be linked in a day by bike providing one is prepared to cover a mile (downhill from Shira to Fyne) of pathless terrain, and some main road. Best therefore to start at the foot of Glen Fyne and cover the main road to Glen Shira early morning to avoid the heaviest traffic and complete the circuit in a clockwise direction. Glen Fyne is 11km (7m) from the main road to the ruin at the end of the track. The above circuit is 46km (29m) including 11km (7m) of main road. The return trip to Allt na Lairige Dam adds 6km (4m).

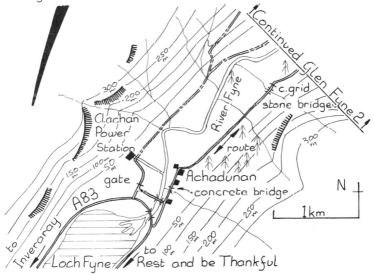

Glen Fyne 2 (Loch Fyne)

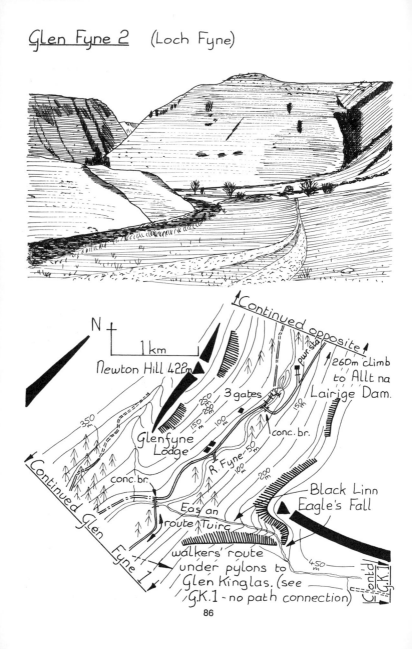

N

1 km

Newton Hill 422m

3 gates

pwr.sta.

260m climb
to Allt na
Lairige Dam.

↑Continued opposite↑

Glenfyne Lodge

250m

200m

150m

100m

conc. br.

R. Fyne

50m

100m

200m

350m

conc. br.

Continued Glen Fyne 1

Eas an
route Tuirc

Black Linn
Eagle's Fall

450m

Cont'd
G.K.1

walkers' route
under pylons to
Glen Kinglas. (see
G.K.1 - no path connection)

86

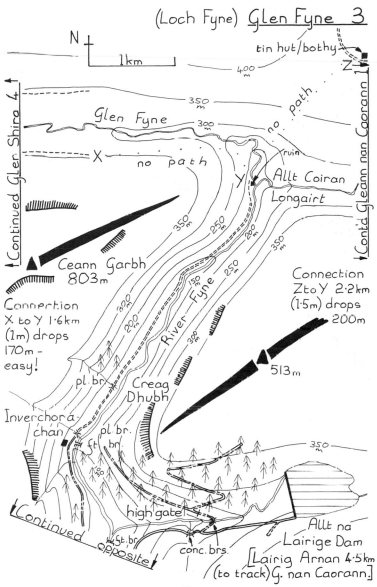

N

1km

tin hut/bothy

400 m

Z

Continued Glen Shira 4

350

no path

Glen Fyne

300

no path

X

no path

ruin

Y

Allt Coiran

Longairt

Cont'd Gleann nan Caorann

350 m

250 m

200 m

250 m

350 m

Ceann Garbh
803 m

Connection
Z to Y 2·2km
(1·5m) drops
200m

200m

350 m

200 m

150 m

River Fyne

300 m

Connection
X to Y 1·6km
(1m) drops
170m –
easy!

pl. br.

Creag
Dhubh

513 m

Inverchora-
chan

pl. br.
br.

ft.

350

high gate

conc. brs.

Allt na
Lairige Dam

Continued
opposite

ft. br.

[Lairig Arnan 4·5km
(to track) G. nan Caorann.]

Glen Shira 1

Glen Shira provides an excellent long mountainbike route through to the head of Glen Fyne. Refer to Glen Fyne 1 for details of the connection. There are two side tracks for those wanting to extend the out-and-back run. For walkers, long treks are possible via Gleann nan Caorann to Glen Falloch (L. Lomond), (approx. 35km or 22miles), as well as Glen Fyne, though much is metalled road in both Glen Shira and Glen Fyne. The start to Lochan Shira dam (far end) is 14km (9m), or 24km (15m) to the ruin in Glen Fyne.

↑Continued Glen Shira 2↑

The geographical similarity between the starting points for Glen Shira and Glen Fyne is worthy of note. Each also has a remnant of old road.

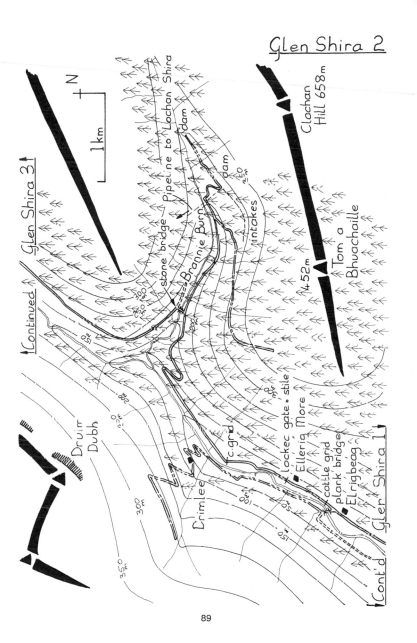

N

1 km

Glen Shira 3

Continued

Druim Dubh

350 m

300 m

Crimlee

250 m

200 m

Lochec gate + stile

c. grid

Elleria More

cattle grid

plank bridge

Elrigbeag

Glen Shira 1

Cont'd

Brannie Burn

stone bridge

Pipeline to Lochan Shira

dam

dam

250m

intakes

150m

300m

100m

50m

Clachan Hill 658m

Tom a Bhuachaille

452m

89

Track X extends for
a further 300m to
a good viewpoint.
Track Y follows a
water conduit-
with inferior
views.

to L. Awe

dam

Y

400m

450m

opposite

quarry
gates

Allt an Stacain

300m

Lochan

350m

350m
400m

Continued

gate
conc. brs.

high gate

X   300m

water intakes   350m   Lochan Sron Mor

N

1 km

dams

excellent
viewpoint

Beinn Ghlas
550m

350m

300m 250m

dam

stone bridge
(above)

Continued Glen Shira 2

from the
dam wall

625m (ish!)

Beinn Bhreac

dams

450 m

400 m

350 m

opposite

Shira

Cont'd

400 m

450 m

Glen Fyne 3

N +

1 km

Cont'd

694 m

Beinn an t-Sidhein

The path to Glen Fyne
starts at point 'Z' after an awkward crossing
of the dam/burn/boggy ground surrounding same. Aim
for a low knoll about a mile ahead (1·5km), following
intakes, after which the path ends. From the knoll
continue on a descending course aiming to join the
river as it turns right (in a further mile) to the ruin.

Ardgartan Forest 1

Ardgartan Forest extends along the north-western shore of Loch Long for some 14km. The northern end is detached due to the main road and this is included with Glen Loin/Loch Sloy. These pages cover the forest south and west of Ardgartan to the tip of the peninsula, a distance of about 12km or 8 miles. Three vital points to note are:- 1/ Forest Enterprise promote an Ardgartan peninsula mountainbike circuit. This is excellent provided it is done clockwise. There is a very rough hill section which is hard work in the recommended direction and involves a "technical" descent (too steep!). If cycling one has to be fit, be prepared to walk/carry, and have good brakes. Your author would not normally advise cycling on such a route, but if Forest Enterprise say it is a bike route who am I to argue? 2/ There is no connection between the Ardgartan and Ardgoil forest tracks despite being only 200m apart. They are separated by impassable crag, the Ardgartan track being some 70m (that's 230ft!) above the Ardgoil track. 3/ The path connecting the tracks at Princes Bridge is very rough and steep - with steps. A short (200m) but awkward carry with bikes. Despite all the above Ardgartan Forest is a great bike ride! - Nearly forgot... there's no shelter either!!

The Environs of Ardgartan

Glen Croe

info centre

picnic spot

gate

A83

Caravan / Camp site

public road

C.C. Site

L. Long

Youth Hostel

to Ardgartan Forest

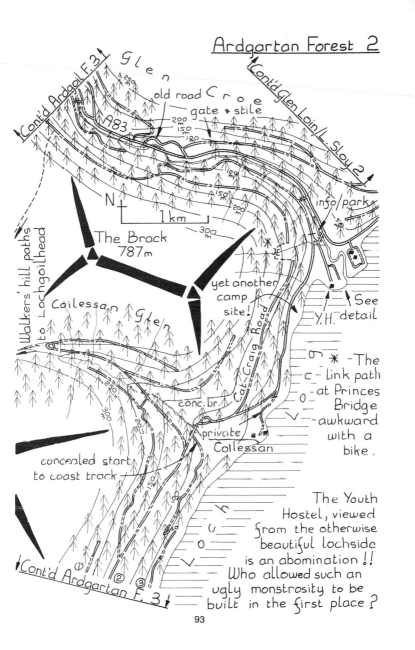

Glen Croe

Cont'd Ardgoil F.3

Cont'd Glen Loin/L. Sloy 2

old road
gate & stile

Cont'd Ardgoil F.3

A83

250 m
200 m
150
180

info/park

N
1 km

150 m
200 m

300 m

The Brack
787m

yet another
camp site!

Coilessan Glen

See Y.H. detail

Walkers' hill paths to Lochgoilhead

σ * — The
c — link path
— at Princes
o — Bridge
ν — awkward
with a
bike.

Cat Craig Road

conc. br.

private
Coilessan

concealed start
to coast track

150
200

300
200

The Youth
Hostel, viewed
from the otherwise
beautiful lochside
is an abomination !!
Who allowed such an
ugly monstrosity to be
built in the first place?

① ② ③

Cont'd Ardgartan F.3

Ardgartan Forest 3

The tip of the peninsula is worth the visit for the views. The rough path, Y, north from Corran Lochan is fine for walking but a 'carry' with a bike. This is, thankfully, the only major obstacle in the Ardgartan peninsula circuit. Walkers may return to Ardgartan by the hill path shown on the previous page map.

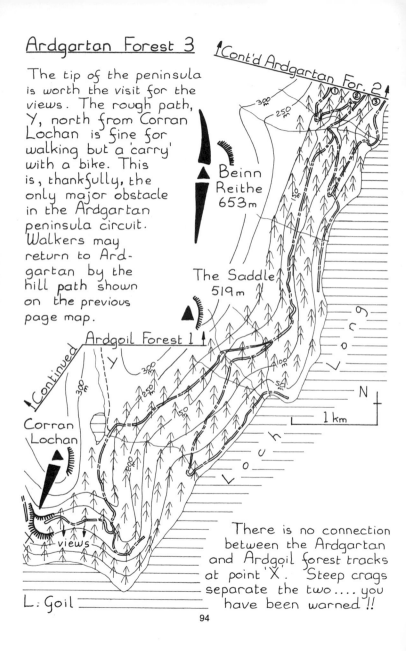

↑Cont'd Ardgartan For. 2→

300 m

250 m

Beinn Reithe 653m

The Saddle 519m

Ardgoil Forest 1 ↑

←Continued

300 m

300 m

250 m

100 m

50 m

Corran Lochan

50 m

200 m

N

1 km

views

X

L: Goil

There is no connection between the Ardgartan and Ardgoil forest tracks at point 'X'. Steep crags separate the two.... you have been warned !!

94

Continued Ardgoil Forest 2

Ardgoil Forest forms the second half of the Ardgartan peninsular circuit, if undertaken in the recommended clockwise direction. After the arduous hill path section at the foot of the map opposite the route is simple – a bit of care is needed in route finding around Lochgoilhead if not visiting the village, and all that remains is the steady climb up Gleann Mor to Rest and be Thankful. The forest road down Glen Croe is preferable to the old road as the latter is populated with livestock. Walkers should note the two hill paths rising from Lochgoilhead to Glen Croe or Coilessan Glen. The complete circuit is some 33km (21 miles). Ardgoil Forest is worthy of exploration on its own but without transport in L'goilhead and Ardgartan, only out-and-back runs are feasible.

<u>Note!</u> The tracks do not link up at X. Steep crags separate them. Danger !!

route

502m
Carn Glas
N
1 km

Stuckbeg
'made' ATV
track-sleep!

rough, vague path

300 m
350 m
300 m

100 m
250 m
200 m
150 m

Clach Bheinn
437m

X

Loch Goil

Continued Ardgartan Forest 3

95

Ardgoil Forest 2

The route through or around Lochgilphead involves about a mile of public road north of the village in order to regain the forest track. The recommended route is shown thus:- ←→ . Note the Loch Goilside road X is connected by rough path only to the route on forest road Y, so keep to the higher track.

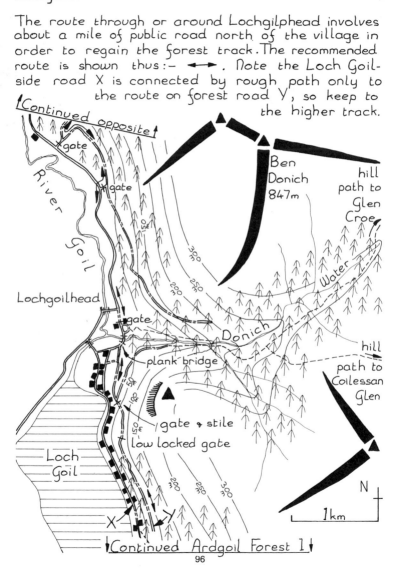

↑Continued opposite↑

River Goil

Ben Donich 847m

hill path to Glen Croe

Lochgoilhead

gate

gate

gate

Donich Water

plank bridge

hill path to Coilessan Glen

gate & stile
low locked gate

Loch Goil

X

N

1km

↓Continued Ardgoil Forest 1↓

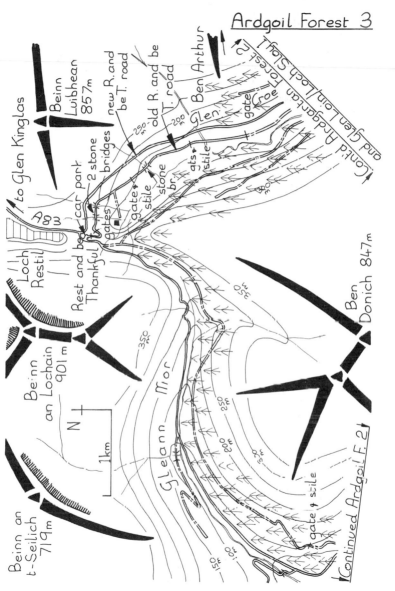

Beinn Luibhean 857m

to Glen Kinglas

A83

Loch Restil

Beinn an Lochain 901m

Beinn an t-Seilich 719m

Rest and be Thankful

car park

2 stone bridges

gates

gate stile

stone br.

gate stile

new R.and be T. road

old R.and be T. road

Glen Croe

gate

ats stile

Ben Arthur

(Contd Ardgarten Forest...

...and Glen Loin/Loch Sloy)

Ben Donich 847m

Gleann Mor

gate & stile

N

1km

250m

200m

150m

100m

350m

300m

250m

200m

150m

100m

350m

Continued Ardgoil F. 2

97

Glen Branter/Glen Shellish 1

The starting point for both Glen Branter and Glen Shellish is the Glenbranter forest car park which also serves as the start for Loch Eck (see next section). Both glens provide high and low level loop tracks and these can be combined to form longer sorties into the forest. Glen Branter, formerly the shorter route of the two, now has a new track extending to Glendaruel, necessitating a long climb on the A886 to return to the start, or transport at both ends. There is no shelter but one can usually descend quickly to base should the need arise. The map opposite gives approximate distances. Considerable climbing is involved reaching the high level tracks.

Continued opposite

Caol Ghleann

Allt a Chaol Ghlinne

150 m

Strondavon

A886

garvie

private

150 m

conc. br.

200 m

gate

250 m

Glendaruel road connection

Duiletter

gate

50 m

100 m

250 m

1km

N

Glen Branter/Glen Shellish 2

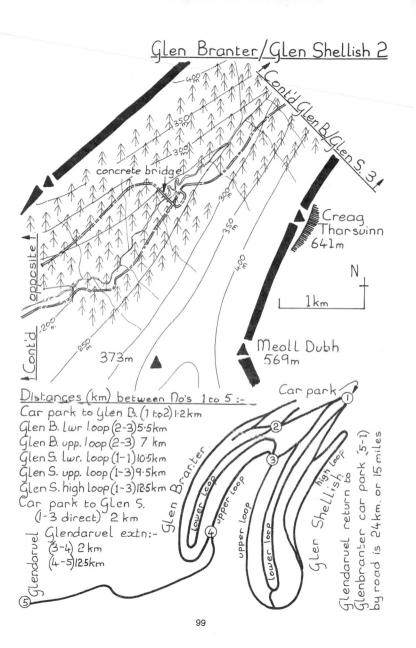

Map labels:
- 400m
- 350m
- 300m
- concrete bridge
- 300m
- 350m
- 400m
- Creag Tharsuinn 641m
- N
- opposite ↑
- 1km
- Cont'd ↑
- 200m
- 250m
- 373m
- Meall Dubh 569m
- Cont'd Glen B/Glen S. 3 ↑

Distances (km) between No's 1 to 5 :-

Car park to Glen B. (1 to 2) 1·2 km
Glen B. Lwr loop (2-3) 5·5 km
Glen B. upp. loop (2-3) 7 km
Glen S. Lwr. loop (1-1) 10·5 km
Glen S. upp. loop (1-3) 9·5 km
Glen S. high loop (1-3) 12·5 km
Car park to Glen S.
　　(1-3 direct) 2 km
　　Glendaruel extn :-
　　(3-4) 2 km
　　(4-5) 12·5 km

Map annotations: Car park ①, ②, ③, Glen Branter, lower loop, upper loop, upper loop, lower loop, Glen Shellish, high loop, ④, Glendaruel, ⑤, Glendaruel return to Glenbranter car park (5-1) by road is 24km or 15 miles

99

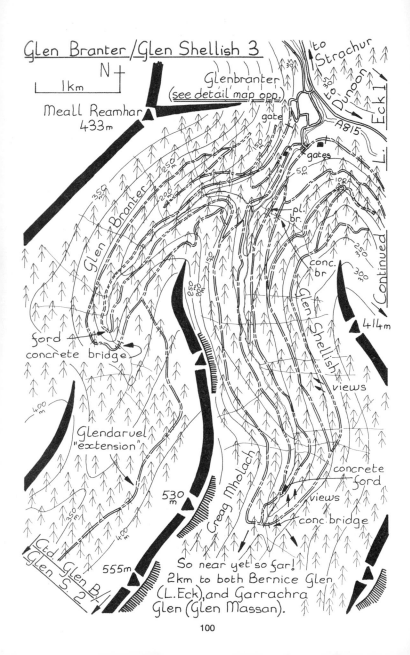

Glen Branter / Glen Shellish 3

N+

1km

Meall Reamhar
433m

Glenbranter
(see detail map opp.)

to Strachur

to Dunoon

L. Eck 1

A815

gate

gates

Glen Branter

pl. br.

conc. br

Glen Shellish

Continued

414m

ford
concrete bridge

views

Glendaruel
"extension"

Creag Mholach

530m

views

concrete ford

conc. bridge

Ctd. Glen B/
Glen S. 2

555m

So near yet so far!
2km to both Bernice Glen
(L. Eck), and Garrachra
Glen (Glen Massan).

100

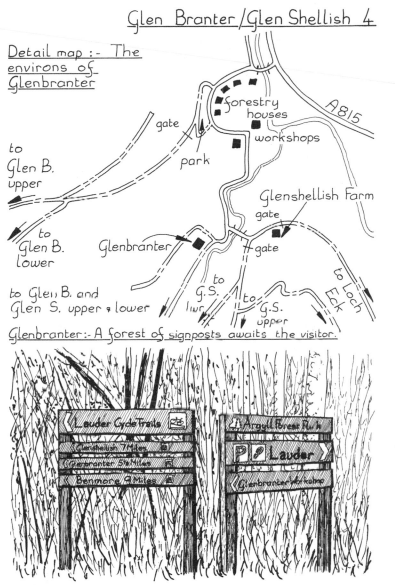

<u>Detail map :- The environs of Glenbranter</u>

A815

forestry houses

workshops

gate

park

to Glen B. upper

to Glen B. lower

Glenshellish Farm

gate

Glenbranter

gate

to Glen B. and Glen S. upper & lower

to G.S. lwr

to G.S. upper

to Loch Eck

<u>Glenbranter:- A forest of signposts awaits the visitor.</u>

Lauder Cycle Trails

Lauder

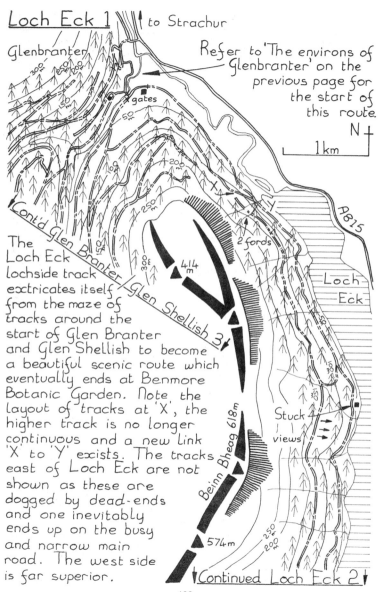

Loch Eck 1

Glenbranter

Refer to 'The environs of
Glenbranter' on the
previous page for
the start of
this route

N

1km

The
Loch Eck
lochside track
extricates itself
from the maze of
tracks around the
start of Glen Branter
and Glen Shellish to become
a beautiful scenic route which
eventually ends at Benmore
Botanic Garden. Note the
layout of tracks at 'X', the
higher track is no longer
continuous and a new link
'X' to 'Y' exists. The tracks
east of Loch Eck are not
shown as these are
dogged by dead-ends
and one inevitably
ends up on the busy
and narrow main
road. The west side
is far superior.

Cont'd Glen Branter / Glen Shellish 3

A815

Loch
Eck

2 fords

414 m

Beinn Bheag 618m

Stuck
views

574m

Continued Loch Eck 2

The Bernice Glen loop should be used if returning to Glenbranter (and combining Glen Shellish with Loch Eck via link track X-Y, left.)

Total distance Glenbranter to Benmore (one way) is 15km or 9.5 miles using the lochside track only. The higher tracks are however also worth exploring. The start/finish of this route at the south or Benmore end is shared with the entrance to the Gardens. (If you are interested in trees this is the place to be!)

Bernice Glen

Bernice

gates

stiles

gate

Loch Eck

A815

conct br

Paper Cave

643m

Cloch Bheinn

cattle grid

gate

N

1 km

Creachan Beag 547m

482m

200

Benmore Botanic Garden

Dunoon

Glen Massan 1

This short route, only 6·5km (4 miles) one way is a pleasant sortie up Glen Massan (as the lower reaches are named - complete with River Massan); and Garrachra Glen (upper reaches - complete with Garrachra Burn). The route may be extended by including 5·5km (3·5 miles) of quiet public road from Invereck, passing the Botanic Garden at Benmore. (Entrance from the main road about a mile south of Loch Eck.)

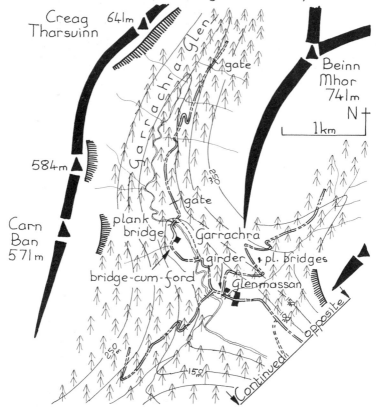

Creag Tharsuinn 641m

Beinn Mhor 741m

N

1km

584m

Carn Ban 571m

gate

gate

plank bridge

Garrachra

girder & pl. bridges

bridge-cum-ford

Glenmassan

250m

250m

150

Continued opposite

104

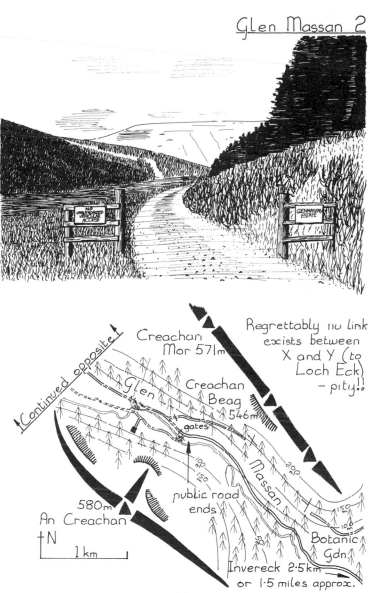

Regrettably no link exists between X and Y (to Loch Eck) – pity!!

Creachan Mor 571m

Creachan Beag 546m

Glen

gates

Continued opposite

Massan

580m
An Creachan

public road ends

Botanic Gdn.

↑N

1 km

Invereck 2·5km or 1·5 miles approx.

105

Glen Fyne 1 (Dunoon)

This route explores the forests of Glen Fyne, which drains the southernmost tip of Cowal, extending to Bishop's Glen above Dunoon. A branch track descends to Innellan but note the track descending to Bullwood is private (and only signposted as such on the main road). Cyclists may use the not-too-busy coast road to complete the 30km (19 mile) circuit from Dunoon. The one-way distance from Ardyne (start of track) to Dunoon is 15 km (9·5 m). There is no shelter other than a quick escape to Innellan.

▲ 522m

350m

▲ 472m

300m

▲ 416m

250m

concrete ford

200m

Corlarach Hill

▲ 418m

▲ 395m

Glen

Corlarach (ruin)

Fyne

100m

locked gate + stile

conc. br.

Linne Mhor Cottage

views to Arran

N

1 km

to Inverchaolain

Ardyne A815

Achafour Farm

to Toward

opposite

Continued

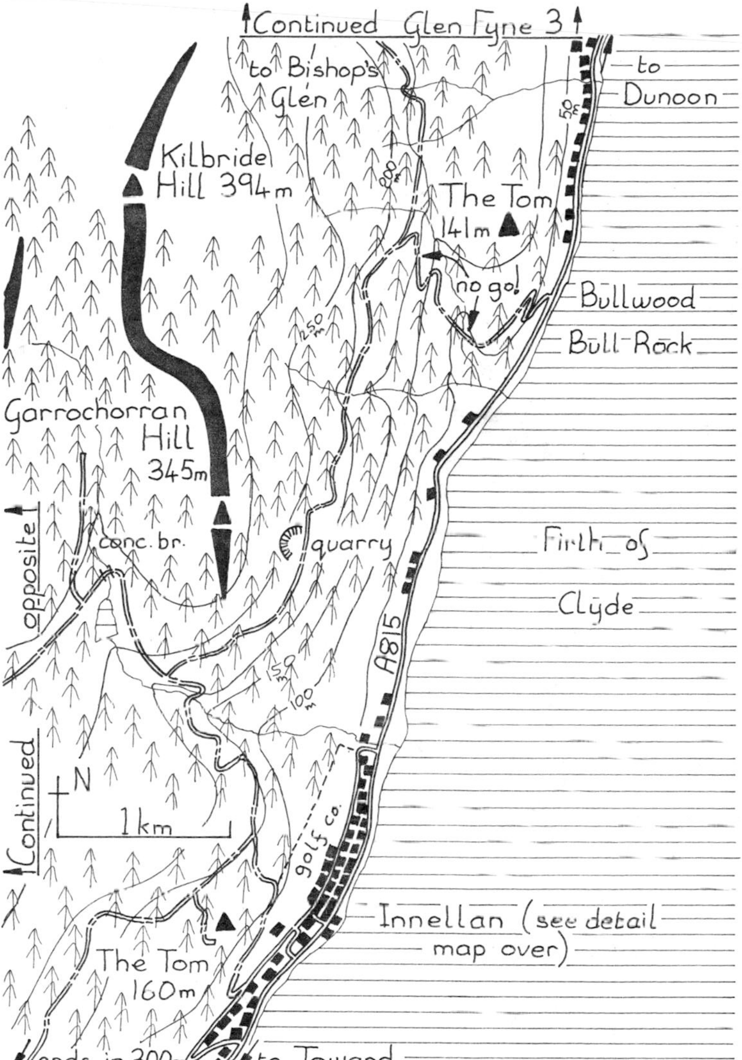
Continued Glen Fyne 3
to Bishop's Glen
to Dunoon
50m
Kilbride Hill 394m
200m
The Tom 141m
no go!
Bullwood
Bull Rock
250m
Garrochorran Hill 345m
opposite
conc. br.
quarry
Firth of Clyde
A815
150m
100m
N
1km
Continued
golf co.
Innellan (see detail map over)
The Tom 160m
ends in 300m
to Toward

Glen Fyne 3 (Dunoon)

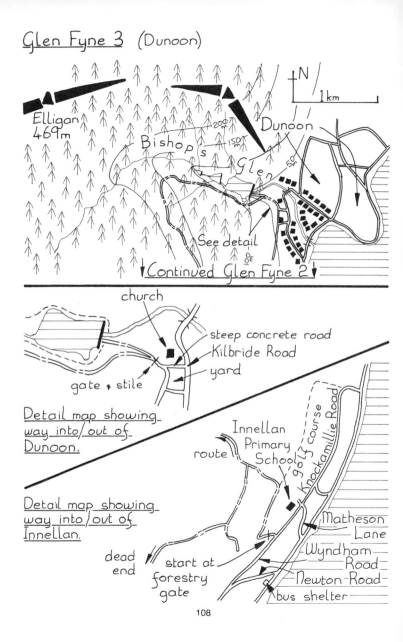

Elligan
469m

Bishop's Glen

200m
150m
50m

Dunoon

N
1km

See detail

Continued Glen Fyne 2

church
steep concrete road
Kilbride Road
yard
gate & stile

Detail map showing
way into/out of
Dunoon.

Innellan
Primary
School
route
golf course
Knockamillie Road

Matheson
Lane
Wyndham
Road
Newton Road
bus shelter

Detail map showing
way into/out of
Innellan.

dead
end
start at
forestry
gate

108

Knapdale and Kintyre

Knapdale and Kintyre

Access:- The way to Knapdale and Kintyre is long and tortuous. The usual route is via Tarbet (Loch Lomond), Inveraray and Lochgilphead, then the long drive south via Tarbert. The shorter and more pleasant approach is to use the Isle of Arran as a stepping stone and the Ardrossan to Brodick and Lochranza to Claonaig (summer only) ferries; certainly the preferred route by bike. The only railway, Campbeltown to Machrihanish is now history.

Accommodation :- Poor. No Youth Hostels, a few camp sites and tourist information only in Campbeltown, supposedly open all year but closed on the Sunday yours truly visited. That's half the weekend! Sorry, but if tourism is to be successful you must try harder. Indeed apart from the Crinan Canal and Knapdale Forest the rest of Knapdale did not appear (to me) to welcome tourists at all. Signposts state:- "Private" ; "Keep Out" ; "Beach for residents only" ; "No entry". OK, we get the message! There is scarcely even a lay-by in Knapdale. Kintyre is better although Campbeltown is more a work-a-day town than a resort. Forest Enterprise seem to be out on their own in welcoming the tourist, they need some support.

Geographical Features :- Knapdale and Kintyre feels very much like an island - it very nearly is of course, and an island 'atmosphere' prevails. Low rolling hills, brilliant yellow gorse and broom and the surrounding blue sea make a very colourful scene (at least if the sun is shining!). The length of the peninsula is deceptive, allow sufficient time for your visit; Strone Glen and Mull of Kintyre are worth the long trek.

Mountains:- None! Island atmosphere maybe, but this is not Skye or Arran.

Rivers:- None! The absence of land mass ensures all water reaches the sea before any decent rivers develop. At least there are no major fords to cross.

Forests:- These are the real reasons for visiting the region, other than to drive aimlessly about adding fumes to the clear Argyll air. Knapdale is the best of course. Several of the privately owned woodlands discourage access so we must be grateful to Forest Enterprise as they are almost alone in allowing Joe Public off the roads. Glen Lussa is next in line in providing miles of traffic free tracks to explore by bike or on foot.

Lochs:- Lussa Loch is the largest sheet of fresh water, though a reservoir. Loch Garasdale is a pleasant, tranquil place. The slightly larger Loch Ciaran, just north of Loch Garasdale unfortunately does not have enough tracks around its shores to make exploration worthwhile.

The Canal:- Once an important commercial link between the Clyde and the open seas to the west and north, the canal still provides a means of avoiding the circumnavigation of the Mull of Kintyre for the many small pleasure boats. The towpath is open to walkers (and cyclists with a licence) thanks to the enlightened attitude of British Waterways, so the canal provides a change from the many forest tracks in the region. The many reservoirs serving the canal provide a network of side-tracks to investigate.

Emergency:- Not really relevant to the tame routes of Knapdale and Kintyre — just take care not to fall in the canal!!

Knapdale and Kintyre Routes 1

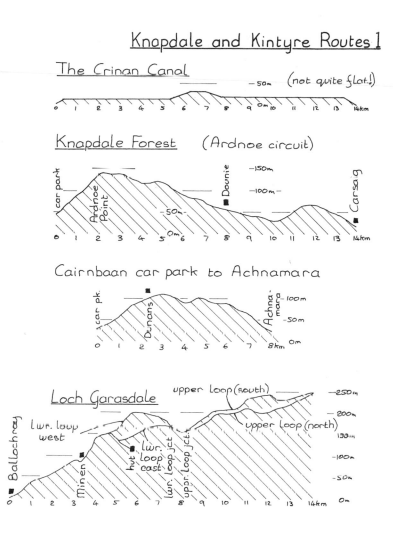

The Crinan Canal

—50m   (not quite flat!)

0 1 2 3 4 5 6 7 8 9 0m 10 11 12 13 14km

Knapdale Forest   (Ardnoe circuit)

car park

Ardnoe Point

—150m

—100m—

Dounie

—50m—

Carsaig

0 1 2 3 4 5 0m 6 7 8 9 10 11 12 13 14km

Cairnbaan car park to Achnamara

car pk.

Dounans

Achnamara

—100m

—50m

0 1 2 3 4 5 6 7 8km 0m

Loch Garasdale

upper loop (south)   —250m

— 200m

lwr. loop west

upper loop (north)

130m

Ballochroy

Minen

hut

lwr. loop east

lwr. loop jct.

upper loop jct.

—100m

—50m

0 1 2 3 4 5 6 7 8 9 10 11 12 13 14km 0m

Knapdale and Kintyre Routes 2

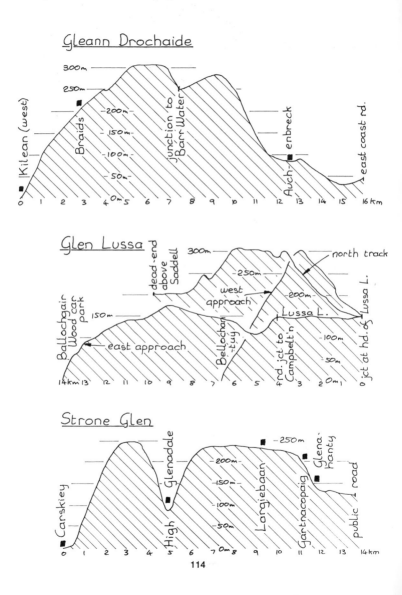

Gleann Drochaide

Glen Lussa

Strone Glen

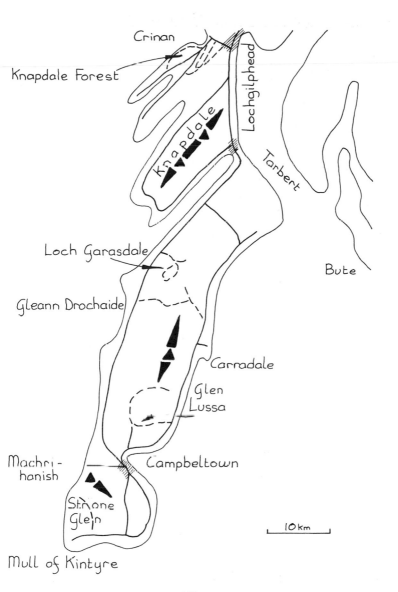

Crinan

Knapdale Forest

Lochgilphead

Knapdale

Tarbert

Loch Garasdale

Gleann Drochaide

Bute

Carradale

Glen
Lussa

Machri-
hanish

Campbeltown

Stⁿone
Glen

10 km

Mull of Kintyre

115

The Crinan Canal
is inextricably linked
with Knapdale Forest
but deserves its own
section as it is separated
from the forest tracks by
a public road. However the
canal links the various forest
tracks, avoiding much use of the road. In order
to cycle on the towpath a licence is obtainable
free of charge from British Waterways Customer
Services on 01923 226422. Their advice leaflet
warns only of possible muddy conditions, though
your author found only a very well maintained
towpath, and of course the usual comment about
cyclists giving way to pedestrians which I know
my well-mannered readers do anyway! Shelter
in the form of civilised cafes lies at each end
of a very easy 14km (or 9 mile) route. Boats
and locks provide a change of scene after the trees.

L13
gate
swing br.
pl. br.
Cairnbaan
Continued L. Glashan 1

Continued opposite

L12
L11
L10 L9
B841 L8 L7 L6 L5

Contd Knapdale Forest

Loch a Bharain serves the highest section of the canal between L8 and L9

50

Crinan Canal

A816

* The canal towpath may be used as a traffic-free link from Lochgilphead most of the way to the start of the forest tracks shown.

N
1km

X = road connection to main road only
Y = road connection to Lochgilphead town centre
Z = road connection to main road thro' Lochgilphead

X
Y

Z

Oakfield Bridge (swing)

below:-
approaching Crinan

Towpath this side may be used between Ardrishaig and Oakfield Bridge

Loch Gilp

L4
L3
L2
L1

Ardrishaig

Knapdale Forest 1

Knapdale Forest provides some of the finest off-road cycling in Argyll, together with numerous forest walks. The section depicted below and opposite covers the Ardnoe Point circuit - 22km or 14 miles including the return on the public road. Best done anti-clockwise for the magnificent views of Jura from above Ardnoe point, return via Tayvallich.

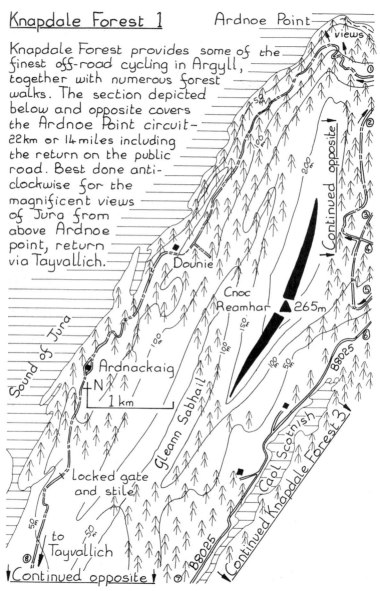

Ardnoe Point

views

①

② Continued opposite

③

④

⑤

⑥

Continued Knapdale Forest 3

B8025

Caol Scotnish

Dounie

Cnoc Reamhar ▲ 265m

Sound of Jura

Ardnackaig

+N
1 km

Gleann Sabhail

locked gate and stile

B8025

to Tayvallich

50

50

⑧

⑦

118

↑Cont'd Crinan Canal 1↑

N

1 km

R. Add

Islandadd Bridge

Cont'd Crinan Canal 1

②opposite

Barr
Bàn
241'm

③Cont'd

South
Leachnaban

Loch Linne

Loch Fidhle

⑤
⑥ B8025

X
gate

Continued Knapdale Forest 3

The
Ardnoe
point
circuit is
best explored
starting from
the car park at
X; – or from the
Crinan Canal via
Islandadd Bridge,
then follow the arrows.

Personal note:-

Your author was
surprised to find a bit
of suburbia (and aggressive
driving!) in Tayvallich. This
seems to rest somewhat un-
easily alongside Loch Sween,
an out-of-character
development that
spoils a typical
west coast
village.

⑧

↑Continued opposite↑

⑦

Carsaig

B8025

Tayvallich

Knapdale Forest 3

The complex array of routes is best divided into four as follows :-
① The Ardnoe circuit
② Rubha Cladh peninsula
③ Rubh an Oib peninsula and L. Coille Bharr (better than ②)
④ Achnamara to Cairnbaan, including the many lochans that feed the Crinan Canal.

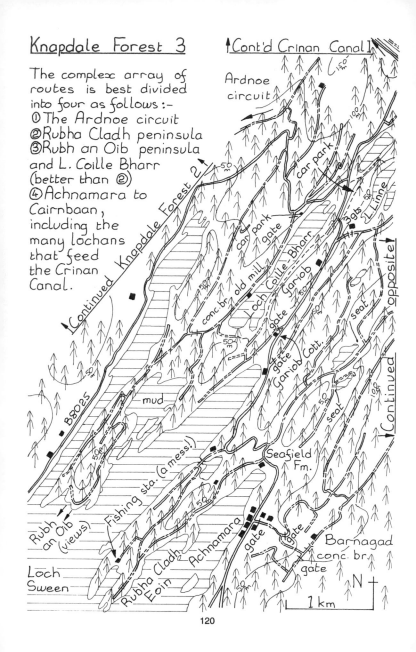

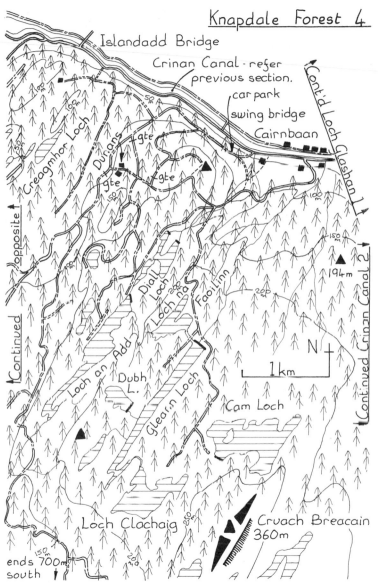

Islandadd Bridge

Crinan Canal - refer previous section.

car park

swing bridge

Cairnbaan

Cont'd Loch Glashan 1

Continued Crinan Canal 2

Creagmhor Loch

Durcans

50m

gte

gte

gte

100

150 m

194m

200

Diall Loch

Loch na

Faoilinn

200

N

1km

Loch an Add

Dubh L.

Glearn Loch

Cam Loch

opposite

Continued

Loch Clachaig

Cruach Breacain
360m

200

150 m

200

ends 700m
south

Knapdale Forest 5

After the complexities of Knapdale Forest your author needs to relax with a few sketches . . . .

The old meal mill Loch Coille-Bharr.

Loch Coille - Bharr.

approaching Bellanoch on the Crinan Canal

. . . . that's better!

Loch Garasdale nestles among the forests of Kintyre about 20km south of Tarbert, access being from the west coast road some 23km or 14m south of Tarbert. After a steep climb the track divides and re-joins before the upper loop of new forest tracks is reached. The preferred direction is arrowed - this takes best advantage of the views and saves the search for the rough track ending at point X which is almost impossible to find from the main track. The round trip including both loops is about 28km or 17m from, and returning to Ballochroy on the main road. There is no shelter and unfortunately no connection to the Gleann Drochaide tracks less than a mile away.

Loch Garasdale fishing hut.

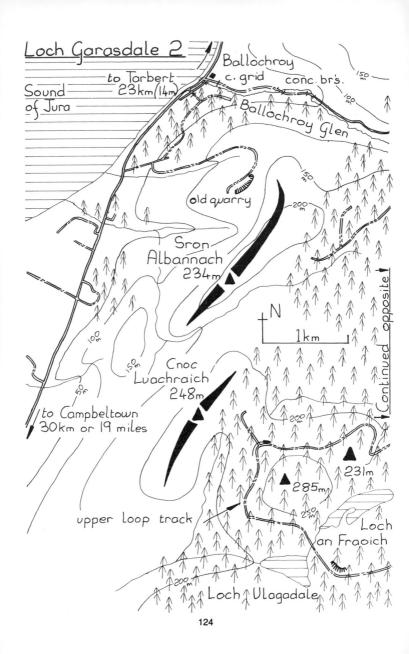

Loch Garasdale 2

Ballochroy
c. grid
conc. br's.

to Tarbert
23km (14m)

Sound
of Jura

Ballochroy Glen

old quarry

Sron
Albannach
234m

N

1km

Cnoc
Luachraich
248m

to Campbeltown
30km or 19 miles

231m

285m

upper loop track

Loch
an Fraoich

Loch Ulagadale

Continued opposite

124

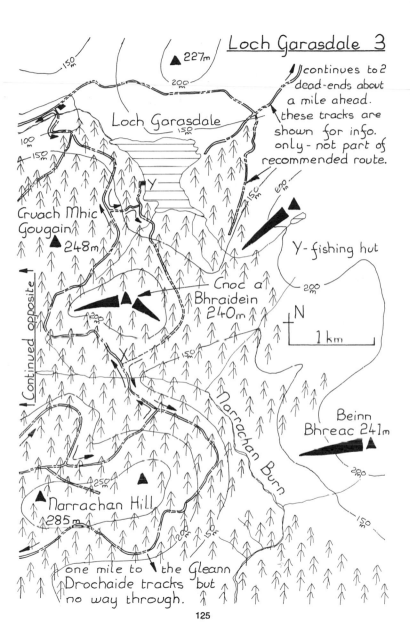

Loch Garasdale 3

continues to 2 dead-ends about a mile ahead. these tracks are shown for info. only - not part of recommended route.

▲ 227m

Loch Garasdale

Cruach Mhic Gougain
▲ 248m

Y - fishing hut

Cnoc a' Bhraidein 240m

N
1 km

Continued opposite

Beinn Bhreac 241m

Narrachan Burn

Narrachan Hill
285m

one mile to the Gleann Drochaide tracks but no way through.

125

Gleann Drochaide 1

The Gleann Drochaide tracks provide an east-west link across the middle of Kintyre, thankfully only open to cyclists and walkers. In the absence of such a road link this makes circular sorties via Claonaig and Clachan, 64km (40m) or Campbeltown, 73km (46m) possible for cyclists or an "across Kintyre" walk of 17km (10·5 miles) for those on foot. The track climbs (twice) to about 300m with a slight descent into the head of Gleann Drochaide at the mid-point. The Drochaide Burn is rejoined at the eastern end when it becomes Carradale Water. There is shelter only at Braids.

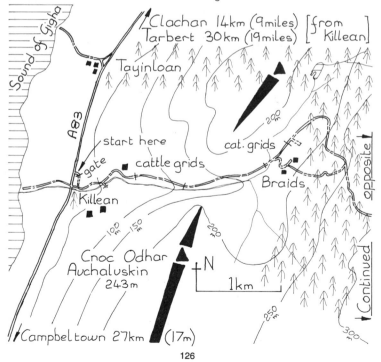

126

The high moorland section of track lies across a treeless expanse maintaining its 300m (1000ft) height for over a mile with good views both east and west.

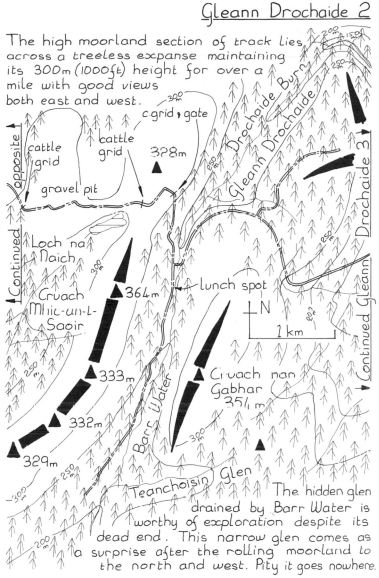

Labels on map:

← Continued opposite

cattle grid

cattle grid

c.grid, gate

gravel pit

328m

Drochaide Burn

Gleann Drochaide

Loch na Maich

Cruach Mhic-un-l-Saoir

364m

lunch spot

N

1 km

333m

332m

329m

Barr Water

Cruach nan Gabhar 354m

Continued Gleann Drochaide 3 →

Teanchoisin Glen

The hidden glen drained by Barr Water is worthy of exploration despite its dead end. This narrow glen comes as a surprise after the rolling moorland to the north and west. Pity it goes nowhere.

Gleann Drochaide 3

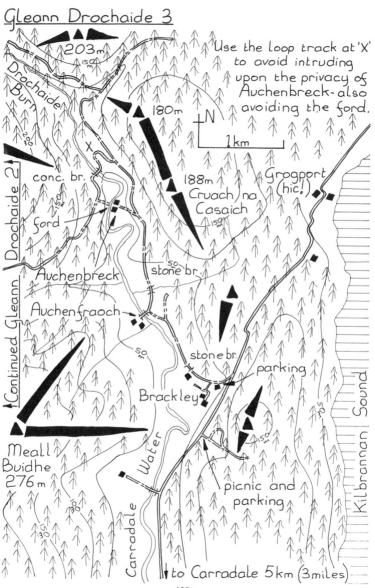

203m

150m

Use the loop track at 'X'
to avoid intruding
upon the privacy of
Auchenbreck - also
avoiding the ford.

Drochaide Burn

180m

N

1km

200 30

X

188m
Cruach na
Casaich

conc. br.

Grogport
(hic!)

150 50

ford

150

Auchenbreck

stone br.

50

Auchenfraoch

50 30

stone br.

parking

Brackley

Meall
Buidhe
276 m

Carradale Water

150 50

picnic and
parking

Kilbrannan Sound

50 30

150 30

↓ to Carradale 5km (3miles)

Continued Gleann Drochaide 2 →

128

Glen Lussa drains the artificially enlarged Lussa Loch via the rather obviously named Glen Lussa Water. The forest tracks link the west coast road via the loch to the minor Lussa Dam road north of Campbeltown and thence to the east coast road via another track. A superb climb runs north, then contours east giving good views over Saddell Glen but sadly leading only to a dead end. The circular trip from Campbeltown including public roads is 42km or 29miles; the one-way (walk?) from Bellochantuy to Ballochgair is 21km or 13m. The north eastern leg is 9km or 6km one way. There is no shelter but there is a picnic table on the lochside – discovered after yours truly had eaten his butties just around the corner sitting on the ground! Glen Lussa is an excellent combination of contour and lochside tracks with a couple of decent climbs thrown in.

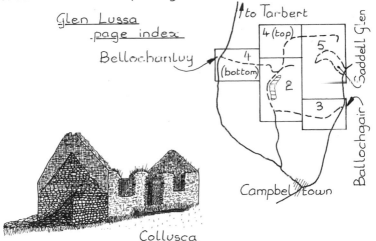

Glen Lussa
page index

Bellochantuy

to Tarbert

4 (top)

5

4 (bottom)

2

3

Saddell Glen

Ballochgair

Campbeltown

Collusca

↑Continued Glen Lussa 4 (top)↑

↑Continued Glen Lussa 4 (bottom)↑

↑Contd Glen Lussa 4 (bottom)↑

▲Meall Buidhe 374m

tin shed

concrete bridge

150

200

250

Bord a Dubh

picnic table

250m

200m

Hughie's Wood

gate

Loch

Stramollach (ruin)

200

250

Corrylach

Lussa

+N

1 km

Sgreadan Hill 397m

60m

Lussa Dam

concrete bridge

cattle grid

Glen

gate ↓ kissing gate

300m

concrete bridge

150m

picnic table

150m

100m

Continued opposite→

Lussa Wtr.

100

300

50

↓to Campbeltown 6km (4 miles)

Forest Enterprise

Ballochgair

[P] [picnic] [information]

to Saddell

locked gate

car pk.

road conn-
ection

Ball"och-
gair

cup marked
rock

Chambered Cairn

B842

Kilbrannan
Sound

Continued opposite

250 m

200 m

150 m

100 m

50

to Campbeltown 8km (5m)

N
1 km

Glen Lussa 4

Map depicting the 150m (500ft) climb above Collusca, NOT connecting with Saddell Glen.

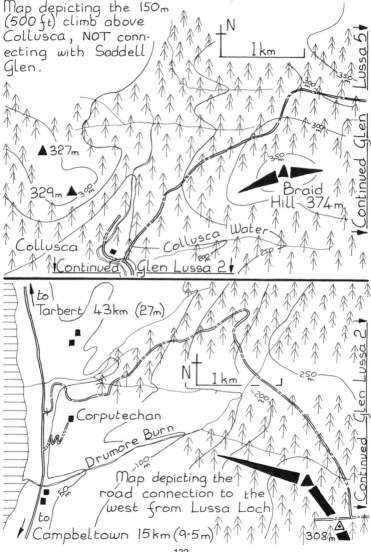

N   1 km

▲327m

329m ▲³⁰⁰m

Braid Hill 374m

350

300
300
350

Continued Glen Lussa 5↑

Collusca

Collusca Water

200

250

↓Continued Glen Lussa 2↓

↑to Tarbert 43km (27m)

N   1 km

250 m

200

■ Corputechan

Drumore Burn

100 m

Map depicting the road connection to the west from Lussa Loch

50 m

↓to Campbeltown 15km (9·5m)

308m ▲

Continued Glen Lussa 2↓

132

▲ Beinn an Turic
454 m

N
1 km

Lussa 4 (top)

350 m
400
250
250
250

views

←Continued Glen

pl. br.

pl. br.

Bord Mor
408 m

200
150
100
gate

150 m

Saddell Water

gate
Saddell Glen

150
100
50
30

gate
gate

Saddell

Saddell Glen
provides a mini-
circular route of
its own, sadly (no
pun intended!) not
connected to either
Lussa Loch (Hughie's
Wood is not a million
miles away) or, more
frustrating, the
contour track
ending just to
the north.

▲ A
Cruach
341 m

250
30

Almost continued
Glen Lussa 3....
about 1km of the
B842 is missing!

Strone Glen 1

The Strone Glen track explores no less than three glens: Strone Glen, Glenadale and Glen Breackerie. The track heads north-east from Carskiey, seemingly oblivious to the lie of the land, running 'across the grain' over hill and glen eventually to reach high moorland before descending through the woods to the minor road. The round trip as above is 22km or 14 miles in length but involves a fair bit of climbing on rough tracks. The clockwise circuit is to be recommended to cyclists as the roughest and steepest sections are then covered downhill. There is shelter (just!) at High Glendale in roofed ruins (and also a pathless 'escape' route to the road at Low Glendale from this point).... This route visits some wild country - away from the procession tackling the tortuous public road to the Mull of Kintyre lighthouse. [This is a good mountainbike ride off-season but being on a public road I am sure my readers don't need a guide book to supplement the map in finding such a famed landmark!]

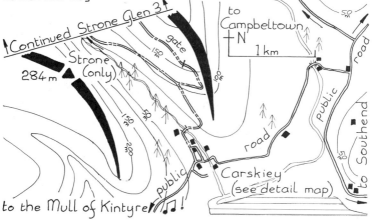

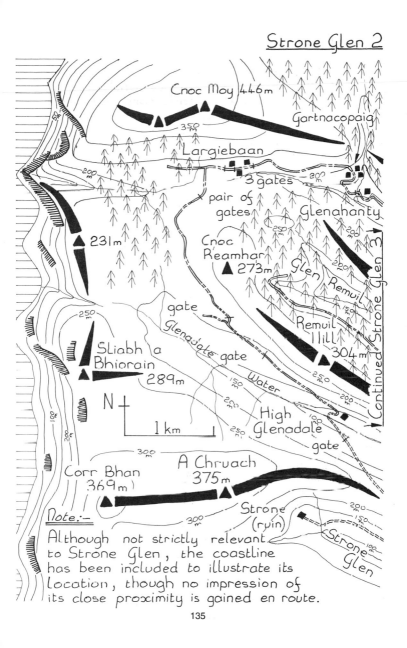

Cnoc Moy 446m

Gartnacopaig

350 m

Largiebaan

50km

200 m

3 gates

200 m

pair of gates

Glenahanty

231m

Cnoc Reamhar

273m

250

200 m

200 m

Glen Remuil

150 m

Remuil Hill

304m

gate

Glenadale

250

gate

Water

150

200 m

250 m

Sliabh a Bhiorain

289m

N

1 km

200

High Glenadale

100

gate

100

300 m

Corr Bhan

369m

A Chruach

375m

300 m

Strone (ruin)

200 m

150 m

100

Strone Glen

Continued Strone Glen 3

<u>Note:-</u>

Although not strictly relevant to Strone Glen, the coastline has been included to illustrate its location, though no impression of its close proximity is gained en route.

135

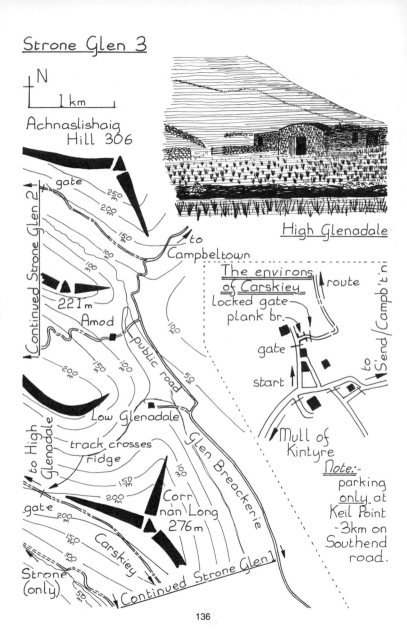

Link Routes

The link routes shown demonstrate how long through routes are made up from the various page maps. Variations can be planned using further adjacent routes but these should provide a basis for extended exploration.

The Ardgartan Peninsula and Loch Lomond

Link Route 1

The circuit of the Ardgartan Peninsula is a 33km or 21mile route providing either a long walk or an arduous cycle ride. See notes on Ardgartan Forest 1 (P92) and Ardgoil Forest 1 (P95) before undertaking this route which is not without its challenges especially with a bike.

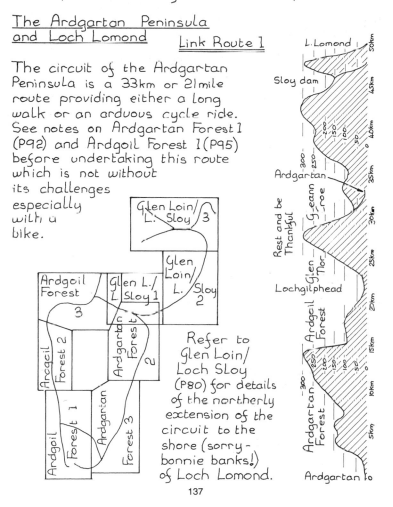

Refer to Glen Loin/ Loch Sloy (P80) for details of the northerly extension of the circuit to the shore (sorry - bonnie banks!) of Loch Lomond.

Oban to Loch Awe circular   Link Route 2

This route provides a fine round trip from just south of Oban to Loch Awe and back. The quiet public roads in Glen Feochan and alongside Loch Scammadale are used but unfortunately these are joined only by either a busy main road or a walkers path (shown dotted below). A fine on/off road cycle ride; the bit of main road is probably worth suffering for the rewards of completing the circuit.   There is too much metalled road for the route to interest the walker:- (Loch Nant and the public roads). Total distance is about 73km or 45 miles depending on variations possible around Gleann Measham and Loch Nant 3 - from, and returning to Oban.

Oban
L. Feochan
Glen Feochan
minor road to Oban
Loch Nant 1
Loch Nant 2
Loch Nant 3
path
L. Scammadale
String of Lorn
Gleann Measham 1
Gleann Measham 2

Oban
minor road
Kilmore
track starts
L. Nant
- 250
- 200
- 150
- 100
- 50
- 0
Inverinan
Gleann Measham
0   5km   10km   15km   20km   25km   30km   35km

Loch Avich
String of Lorn
- 300
- 250
- 200
- 150
- 100
- 50
- 0
Loch Scammadale
main road/ Loch Feochan
Kilmore
minor road
Oban
35km   40km   45km   50km   55km   60km   65km   70km

Link Route 3   Circuit of Ben Cruachan

If the main road section is covered early in the morning
this circuit makes a fine mountainbike ride (or excellent
walk if restricted to Glen Kinglass only). The full circuit
is 82km (51m) and probably the best mixed on/off road
route in this guide. Glen Kinglass is arguably the best
low level through walk though at 35km (22m), or 43km
(29m) from Taynuilt to Bridge of Orchy railway stations
it is a long one! Walkers (only) have the option of
the lochside path to Glen Etive whilst both walkers
and cyclists have a multitude of
long routes north and
east of
Victoria
Bridge:-
See Book
3-The
Glens of
Rannoch.

Book 3 !!

Glen Etive path

Glen Kinglass 5

Glen Kinglass 6

Glen Kinglass 7

Glen Kinglass 4

Glen Kinglass 3

Glen Kinglass 2

Glen Orchy 2

Glen Orchy 1

Victoria Bridge

ATV trail

Ben Cruachan

'B' road

Pass of Brander

Dalmally

Glen Orchy

to Tyndrum

Taynuilt

Br. of Awe

139

Inveraray to Glen Falloch   Link Route 4

Glen Shira to Glen Fyne is a circuit suited to the cyclist due to the metalled section in Glen Shira which makes this glen unattractive to the walker. The short pathless link is on shortish grass and downhill if done Shira to Fyne. Total circuit including main road is 46km (29m). Gleann nan Caorann/Glen Fyne is best undertaken as a walk (22km or 14miles) due to the rougher link between the two (this link is down hill heading from Caorann to Fyne). Glen Shira and Gleann nan Caorann are dominated by hydro schemes so scenically Glen Fyne wins.

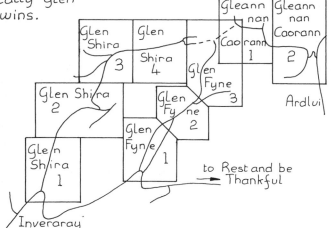

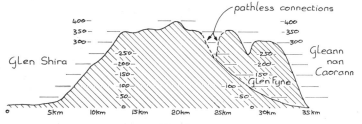

Book 5 complete, little did I think how the series would develop when I wrote The Cairngorm Glens six years ago. This labour of love finds me working my way northwards. Next is The Great Glen, Monadhliath and Moray, then Book 7, south and east of the Cairngorms, before a taste of real wilderness not seen since Rannoch as I head north through Wester Ross, Easter Ross and on into Sutherland – wild country indeed !.... I have enjoyed Argyll, its sea lochs and its contrasts. Knapdale and Kintyre with its island-like 'feel' and apparent reluctance to accept the visitor. Perhaps, having seen the changes the boating crowd have made around Crinan, this is understandable; not that I dislike 'boaters'! Perhaps I dislike out-of-character change too much! North of the peninsula is an area of forest, sea loch and mountains, all crammed in, leaving little room for true wilderness. This region has some of the finest peaks in Scotland, around Glen Etive and towards Glencoe, and all lie within too-easy reach of the roads. I prefer to savour the long wild glens on the approach to the mountains, not the "park-and-bag-a-Munro" type of walking now so prevalent. The Scottish mountains deserve better. I digress, this guide is about the Glens, I do hope glen-bagging doesn't become the latest fad. The outdoors is not some vast gymnasium with things to be 'done' and ticked off in a book. Surely, the object of enjoying the outdoors is to rid oneself of the regimentation and urgency of our working lives, not to re-introduce it. Now we have mobile 'phones and satellite navigation in the mountains – when self-reliance (and getting away from the 'phone!) used to be the reasons for being there. Let's keep a wary eye on our self-destruction of our objectives in the few wild places left.... Enough of my ramblings for now!

PRINTED BY CARNMOR PRINT & DESIGN
95/97 LONDON ROAD, PRESTON, LANCASHIRE